BY HIS STRIPES

THE UNANSWERED QUESTION ABOUT WHY THE WOMAN APPROACHED JESUS FROM BEHIND...

The exact reason for her change in approach has not been established, but different reasons have been given.

In 1 Peter 2:24, we read, "Who his own self bare our sins in his own body on the tree that we, being dead to sins, should live unto righteousness: by whose stripes ye were healed." But what do these "stripes" of Jesus really mean?

This theological text examines the relationship between Jesus, who has our salvation written on his back through the wounds he suffered for our sake, and the bleeding woman he heals after she touches the hem of his cloak in Luke 8:40–48.

By His Stripes: The Healing of the Church asks readers to consider this relationship in more depth and what it means for Christians today. After reading this book, you will learn the following:

- Why the woman approached Jesus from behind to touch the hem of his garment
- Why the woman was in a state of bleeding
- How to touch the stripes of Jesus for healing
- Who the woman in the picture of Jesus and Jairus daughter was
- Why the woman came between Jairus daughter's illness and her awakening
- How Jesus is healing the ailing church

The church may seem to be occupied with the work of God, but which God are they working for? The god of the world or the God of life? The church today has surrounded itself with things that are meant for the world, not for the church. The church has lost perspective.

By examining the significance of the passages above, readers will gain a new perspective on these and other aspects of Christianity.

What is the significance of the woman touching Jesus' servant-hood garment?

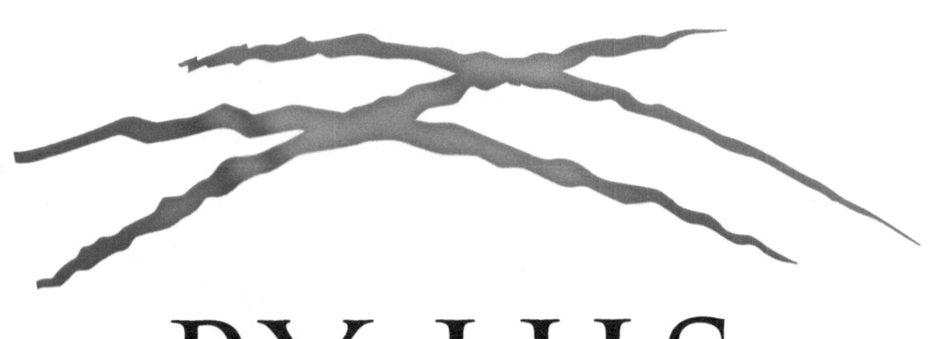

BY HIS STRIPES

THE HEALING OF THE CHURCH

EUNICE FORSON

BY HIS STRIPES
THE HEALING OF THE CHURCH

Printed in the United Kingdom

Published by The Seed Publications

For information please contact the author via email: themustardseed337@gmail.com

Visit theseeddotblog.com

ISBN 978-1-9160913-0-6 paperback
ISBN 978-1-9160913-1-3 eBook

Cover and Interior Design by:
Chris Treccani
www.3dogcreative.net

The Mustard Seed
MINISTRIES

This book is dedicated to the woman who taught me
how to touch the stripes of Jesus:

My Beloved Mother

Augustina Cann-Barnieh

To my children

Honora and William Mensah Bonsu

And to the woman who gave me the reason to stand firm and
trust in God and to let others know about Christ. Your note
was received. Thank you for your word of encouragement,
the gift and your prayers. God bless you. Just as your message
began "Always BELIEVE something wonderful IS ABOUT
TO happen" and ended:

My sister-in-Christ

Debra

CONTENTS

PREFACE

On October 18, 2018, I attended a women's conference in Dallas, Texas. The message that dominated the conference was from the Book of Luke 8:43-48. It was about the woman with the issue of blood, but the unanswered question throughout the various teachings was in verse 44 (She *came up in the crowd behind Jesus and touched the edge of his cloak, and her bleeding stopped at once [GNT]*). Why did this woman approach Jesus from behind? This is the question needing an answer, and only vague ones have been given so far. The exact reason for the woman's change in the direction of approaching Jesus has not been established, but different reasons have been given.

On October 20, 2018, during the morning glory session of the conference, as we were praying, I called upon God for healing. I believed I was healed according to 1 Peter 2:24. His word says that by the stripes of Jesus, I am healed. With great confidence, I stood on the authority of God's word and declared my healing. There and then, God revealed to me the concept of the stripes of Jesus.

The Lord says I shouldn't just verbally declare 1 Peter 2:24, but I have to touch the stripes of Jesus. It is one thing to declare the healing by Jesus' stripes and another to physically touch the stripes that heal. As Apostle Thomas was told in the Bible to put his finger in Jesus' hands and see, and reach out his hand and put into Jesus' side to remove the doubt in his eyes, likewise Jesus is also teaching you to touch His stripes for healing. It was at that instant God gave me this revelation to the concept of the stripes of Jesus and the healing of the woman with the issue of blood.

Jairus' Daughter and the Woman Who Touched Jesus' Cloak

When Jesus returned to the other side of the lake, the people welcomed him, because they had all been waiting for him. Then a man named Jairus arrived; he was an official in the local synagogue. He threw himself down at Jesus' feet and begged him to go to his home, because his only daughter, who was twelve years old, was dying.

As Jesus went along, the people were crowding him from every side. Among them was a woman who had suffered from severe bleeding for twelve years; she had spent all she had on doctors, but no one had been able to cure her. She came up in the crowd behind Jesus and touched the edge of his cloak, and her bleeding stopped at once. Jesus asked, "Who touched me?"

Everyone denied it, and Peter said, "Master, the people are all around you and crowding in on you."

But Jesus said, "Someone touched me, for I knew it when power went out of me." The woman saw that she had been found out, so she came trembling and threw herself at Jesus' feet. There in front of everybody, she told him why she had touched him and how she had been healed at once. Jesus said to her, "My daughter, your faith has made you well. Go in peace."

While Jesus was saying this, a messenger came from the official's house. "Your daughter has died," he told Jairus; "don't bother the Teacher any longer."

But Jesus heard it and said to Jairus, "Don't be afraid; only believe, and she will be well."

(Luke 8:40–50; GNT)

Submission to Masters

Servants, be submissive to your masters with all fear, not only to the good and gentle, but also to the harsh. For this is commendable, if because of conscience toward God one endures grief, suffering wrongfully. For what credit is it if, when you are beaten for your faults, you take it patiently? But when you do good and suffer, if you take it patiently, this is commendable before God. For to this you were called, because Christ also suffered for us, leaving us an example, that you should follow His steps:

"Who committed no sin,
Nor was deceit found in His mouth";

who, when He was reviled, did not revile in return; when He suffered, He did not threaten, but committed Himself to Him who judges righteously; who Himself bore our sins in His own body on the tree, that we, having died to sins, might live for righteousness—by whose stripes you were healed. For you were like sheep going astray, but have now returned to the Shepherd and Overseer of your souls.

(1 Peter 2:18-25 NKJV)

The Sin-Bearing Messiah

Who has believed our report?

And to whom has the arm of the Lord been revealed?

For He shall grow up before Him as a tender plant, and as a root out of dry ground. He has no form or comeliness; and when we see Him, there is no beauty that we should desire Him.

He is despised and rejected by men, a Man of sorrows and acquainted with grief.

And we hid, as it were, our faces from Him; He was despised, and we did not esteem Him.

Surely He has borne our griefs and carried our sorrows; yet we esteemed Him stricken, smitten by God, and afflicted.

But He was wounded for our transgressions, He was bruised for our iniquities; the chastisement for our peace was upon Him, and by His stripes we are healed.

All we like sheep have gone astray; we have turned, every one, to his own way; and the Lord has laid on Him the iniquity of us all.

(Isaiah 53:1-6; NKJV)

CHAPTER ONE

By His Stripes

> *"Who Himself bore our sins in His own body on the tree, that we, having died to sins, might live for righteousness—by whose stripes you were healed." (1 Peter 2:24)*

The Lord said you shouldn't just pray to be healed by the stripes of Jesus, but you should touch His stripes to receive your healing. There is a difference between "praying for" things to happen and physically "touching" these things. You pray for things you cannot access, but you touch things that are accessible to you. This is what you do when you pray to the Lord for healing. The word "healing" is for those who need the Lord God in their lives.

HEALING

The meaning of "healing" includes:

- A <u>process</u> in which an organism's health is <u>restored</u>.
- A process of returning to health; the restoration of structure and function of injured or diseased tissue.
- To set right; repair
- To <u>recover</u> from an illness or injury.

Healing is a process, and "process" is defined as:

1. A series of actions or steps taken in order to achieve a particular result.
2. A series of things which happen naturally and result in a biological or chemical change.

Healing involves a process, and this process entails taking steps into your healing. You cannot get healed by sitting in one place. You will need to move from your state of unbelief to a state of belief and take steps into your healing. You have to be a believer, shifting from faithless to faith-ridden! In order to get to the faith level, you will have to pass through different levels of trials—going through the land with no cure, losing all your money to healers, crowding in on Jesus, to coming behind from the crowd to receive healing.

The reason the Lord said you do not just verbally declare the healing stripes of Jesus, but touch those stripes to receive your healing is that you cannot stay in one place to receive healing. You need to move according to the word of God. Healing does not come to man as healing is not physical. Man has to reach out to it. You need to declare it, but you have to take actions in order to be healed:

- You need to serve the Lord to receive your healing.
- You need to show sincerity to be healed.
- You need to show love to receive your healing.
- You need to pronounce His word to receive His healing.
- You need to be law abiding to receive His healing.

You do not receive healing from Jesus just because you called out the name of Jesus. Jesus heals us from within, and that involves dedication and love. It entails you being committed to Him. It demands a whole lot, so do not deny yourself of healing just by throwing words in the air, but commit to the Lord for healing. Steps need to be taken to get healed, and these steps are a dedication to the Lord and love. So, you see, love conquers all. In our healing, we need love in our soul. You cannot get healed without love. Jesus is intertwined in our healing. The steps to be taken are what the woman with the issue of blood took to receive her healing. She took a leap of faith. She came up behind from the crowd to touch the hem of Jesus' garment. She committed to Jesus and her healing.

Steps need to be taken in order to get healed and in this book, the Lord has laid out the steps required for your healing—from the daughter of Jairus' sickness to the woman with the issue of blood and then to the awakening of Jairus' daughter. There is a process! You cannot hop over this process and get healed. Healing needs your attention and dedication. You need to learn from Jairus' daughter case to tap into your healing. You need to acknowledge your need for healing; then the Lord will heal you. If you do not, you will wander around forever in the land looking for healing as the woman did in the text. You need to recognize within yourself that you need healing, and until you do so, healing will not come to you. If you do not recognize your need, you will die in your sorrow. That is the process!

Steps to be taken:

1. Recognizing your need for healing.
2. Making the right decision.
3. Giving a decision to your thoughts.
4. Taking actions for your thought—rise and make a move (need to look out for the healer—reach out to Him).
5. Giving that thought a goal.
6. Achieving that goal.

These are the steps to be taken in order to achieve your healing. You cannot achieve your healing without making decisive moves. You need to take steps into your healing, and these steps involve commitment, dedication, love, and endurance (to live according to His will). You need these to survive the hardship of healing. You cannot heal without hardship because on the back of Jesus are His stripes, and these stripes are a remembrance of His courage and dedication to His cause. In order to be healed, you need courage and dedication from Jesus; you need to share in His suffering. This is why the woman touched Jesus' garment for her healing. She needed that power that had been granted to Jesus to withstand all the hardship attached to the cross to get healed. She understood the power that Jesus possessed and made a reach for it in order to be healed. She grabbed onto that power to get healed, and she received her healing instantly.

Question: How do you grab on to the power on Jesus to get healed?

Healing here refers to the restoration of everything lost due to the bleeding. The word of God says healing is good for the soul. He resurrects and restores us to normal health. Healing brings us back to God. So, the word "healing" in the Bible is about restoration by the Lord. Jesus heals our souls.

Healing is what God is doing with us; setting us right with Him. God brought His Son to us on earth to achieve that. He prayed over our lives and brought us together. God healed the ground that He has cursed, including healing the nation of God. He brought healing to us and restored us into His Kingdom. Healing the sick is one of His roles as a deliverer. Jesus came to heal the ground God cursed.

He heals the broken-hearted and
bandages their wounds.
(Psalms 147:3; GNT)

And He was handed the book of the prophet Isaiah. And when He had opened the book, He found the place where it was written: "The Spirit of the Lord is upon Me, Because He has anointed Me to preach the gospel to the poor; He has sent Me to heal the broken-hearted, to proclaim liberty to the captives and recovery of sight to the blind, to set at liberty those who are oppressed.
(Luke 4:17–18; NKJV)

"I do not accept glory from human beings, but I know you. I know that you do not have the love of God in your hearts. I have come in my Father's name, and you do not accept me; but if someone else comes in his own name, you will accept him. How can you believe since you accept glory from one another but do not seek the glory that comes from the only God?"
(John 5:4–44)

Healing and Restoration

"Healing" and "Restoration" go hand in hand. Restoration leads to healing.

"For I will restore health to you and heal you of your wounds,' says the Lord, 'because they

*called you an outcast saying: "This is Zion; No
one seeks her."*
(Jeremiah 30:17; NKJV)

The nail mark in Jesus' hands and feet, the hole in His side where they pierced him, every wound on His body, and every suffering endured on His journey to and on the cross are for the benefit of man to be healed. Every mark on Jesus' body has a meaning and purpose to it. Jesus used His body to defend mankind and to give man salvation.

It stands for His Sovereignty. Jesus says in the Book of Matthew 11:28, "Come to me, all you who are weary and heavy burden, and I will give you rest" (NIV).

Healing is in the stripes of Jesus!

Touch the wounds of Jesus for your healing!

Jesus' Journey to the Cross

For the Word says:

*"But the angel said to her, "Do not be
afraid, Mary; you have found favour with God.
You will conceive and give birth to a son, and
you are to call him Jesus. He will be great and
will be called the Son of the Most High. The
Lord God will give him the throne of his father David, and he will reign over Jacob's
descendants forever; his kingdom will never*

end." "How will this be," Mary asked the angel, "since I am a virgin?"

The angel answered, "The Holy Spirit will come on you, and the power of the Most High will overshadow you. So the holy one to be born will be called the Son of God."
(Luke 1:30-35; GNT)

*"She gave birth to her first son, **wrapped him in cloths** and laid him in a manger—there was no room for them to stay in the inn."*
(Luke 2:7; NIV [emphasis added])

"Jesus knew that the Father had given him complete power; he knew that he had come from God and was going to God. So he rose from the table, took off his outer garment, and tied a towel around his waist. Then he poured some water into a washbasin and began to wash the disciples' feet and dry them with the towel around his waist." **(John 13:3-5; GNT)**

"Then Pilate took Jesus and had him whipped. The soldiers made a crown out of thorny branches and put it on his head; then they put a purple robe on him and came to him and said,

"Long live the King of the Jews!" And they went up and slapped him (**John 19:1-3; GNT**)

When the chief priests and the Temple guards saw him, they shouted, "Crucify him! Crucify him!" Pilate said to them, "You take him, then, and crucify him. I find no reason to condemn him." The crowd answered back, "We have a law that says he ought to die, because he claimed to be the Son of God."
(John 19:6-7; GNT)

Jesus answered, "You have authority over me only because it was given to you by God. So the man who handed me over to you is guilty of a worse sin."
(John 19:11; GNT)

"After they had mocked him, they took off the robe and put his own clothes on him. Then they led him away to crucify him."
(Matthew 27:31; NIV)

They shouted back, "Kill him! Kill him! Crucify him!" Pilate asked them, "Do you want me to crucify your king?" The chief priests answered, "The only king we have is the Emperor!"

Then Pilate handed Jesus over to them to be crucified. So they took charge of Jesus. He went out, carrying his cross, and came to "The Place of the Skull," as it is called (In Hebrew it is called "Golgotha.")."
(John 19:15 -17; GNT)

The Journey to the Cross

1. Jesus triumphant entry from Bethany.
2. Preached in the temple.
3. Cleansed the temple.
4. The Last Supper (Mark 14: 15 and Luke 22: 12).
5. Descended into the Kidron valley to Gethsemane, the oil press.
6. Jesus arrested in Gethsemane by a crowd led by Judas Iscariot.
7. Jesus before high priests.
8. Denied by Peter.
9. Jesus condemned.
10. Jesus carries the cross to Calvary.
11. Jesus is stripped and nailed to the cross.
12. Jesus died on the cross.
13. Jesus was buried in the tomb.

The promises of Genesis 3:15 are fulfilled in Jesus' journey to and on the cross. Jesus crushed the head of the serpent, and the serpent bruised his heels; both were achieved to and on the cross—the bruising and the healing. The stripes of Jesus were obtained by the whipping of the Word of God (Jesus) by the crowd crushing in on Him. Every point in (step of) His journey was for the sake of man. The world brought the Word of God to judgment, and through the judgment, He obtained the stripes on His back. Jesus suffered extreme torture inflicted on any human being.

These stripes were obtained with man in mind as a route for man to gain his freedom. The stripes were obtained so that man will find his way to Christ, the Deliverer. He received all these stripes so that man will seek Him instead of the world. He needs not to watch himself but to follow the path that has been set before him.

God gave His word at the beginning of creation as the Father of all living. He gave His word to the world that one day, He will come and rescue man from all that we are seeing; the evil world. He gave man His word as the Resurrection King, who will one day come to bring us peace. He came to us in His garment, reigning in our lives. He came in humility and accepted our sin on Him—He wore our sins on Him by taking on the body of man. He wore the flesh of Man. He came to us as the Child born to the Virgin Mary (earth) and will be given to us as a Son. God took Him from the ground and brought life to Him. God took on the nature of man. He took on our worldly faith and shredded it into pieces when He went to the cross. He destroyed our faith in the enemy and made us free from the hands of the wicked one. He took on the grave.

God took on the nature of mankind to save His creation (man). God came to us on earth in the form of man, and as He wandered the earth with us, He proclaimed His will. God took off His royal garment and put on the garment of servanthood to serve us. That is what He came to earth with, for Him to destroy the works of the enemy. With that garment on, He went through His journey to the cross to destroy the nature of flesh. This flesh was taken on by God in the form of Jesus, and this flesh was indirectly destroyed by man. Man destroyed the flesh without knowingly doing it. Man fought and destroyed the very flesh that was fighting against him.

Jesus was the "enmity" (Genesis 3:15) put between the serpent and the woman. He became the carrier of the flesh, a barrier between the woman and the serpent. Jesus carried on Himself the very flesh that was destroying man and allowed man with the power given to him (John 19:11) by God to destroy this flesh they are carrying. Jesus took on the strength of man to wage that war, and as the war was over, He gave back the flesh to the earth. He went to the grave and resurrected on the third day without the sinful flesh. He broke the curse of the flesh—the covering on man. Every wound on His body is for the salvation of man.

God did not bring man into this world (Genesis 3: 22-24) to be saved by the devil but brought man into the world to defend His nature. God brought man into this world to know how to defend themselves; therefore, the purpose of the slain lamb to banish our sins. You have to be in control of the flesh.

Jesus suffered the way He did to the cross for your sake to conquer the world. Jesus broke down the flesh as He journeyed through His sufferings to dying on the cross (John 19: 1–17).

Jesus and the Cross

Jesus took on the body of a man and broke it on the cross to bring salvation to man. He reserved the body of Christ for that of man. He claimed our salvation on the cross to bring us peace. So, the touching of the garment is a representation of our peace on the cross. On that cross which is our salvation, Jesus brought us out from the grip of the enemy. The enmity God spoke about is that of the cross. God placed the cross in-between man and the devil.

On the cross, Jesus Christ died for our salvation with His flesh all torn in pieces for our sake, and through those stripes, the struggle and pain, we are saved. He did not only die on the cross, but He has carried the cross on His shoulder till now to bring you favor. He made it to the cross with your love in His heart and with that love, He made it to the cross. He did not only carry the cross at heart but also carried your love in His heart. And with that love, He set you free from the devil.

The journey to the cross was inevitable, but the journey on the cross was crucial. It was for man to seek his independence from the evil one. Jesus bought us peace for going to the cross. He taught us how to go to the cross with a heavy heart and come out victorious. Jesus went to the cross with a lot of misunderstandings but came out as the hero in our day. He fought for mankind and came out victorious. The cross is there for man and man for the cross. Jesus achieved His purpose on the cross, so what is the cross in terms of Jesus' journey?

The cross is what Jesus carried on Himself to the grave. He broke this body and buried it in our name. He sought revenge on what the enemy did to man by bringing the very thing that the enemy hates to victory. He brought man to victory. He tore down this body into pieces in exchange for the love that He has for man.

In order to follow Jesus as a true worshipper, you must follow Him in your shredded body. You must put on His pain and trauma. You cannot earn His love without His trauma; you must go through it. You must suffer as He did by giving up the flesh (the desires). You will have to break those desires for the desires of God. Jesus relinquished His desires as a man for that of Christ. That is where people confuse their desires for lust. Jesus changes the heart of man to the heart of God.

The cross is to be carried, but by who? Who is strong enough to carry the cross? The cross comes with all sorts of trials; are we bold to carry it? The cross of Jesus had all sorts of things written on it; are you bold to carry it to the end? Because you will have to kill your flesh on that cross and bury it. The cross is there for man to judge his journey. It measures your strength and ability; your capability of getting things done in the kingdom.

The cross is there for pain; to endure pain in our walk. Will you be able to endure that pain that the woman went through, walking around twelve years with an issue of blood; the rejection, humiliation, failure, abandonment, and cruelty? Will you be able to endure her pain? She labored around in pain until she came face to face with Jesus. She touched His garment to get healed and immediately, she was healed. The woman knew what she was doing and capable of doing. She walked around in pain, but she came out of her pain immediately after touching Jesus' garment. She suffered on her journey and never gave up. She bled along her journey and never threw in the towel. She sought all help, but no one helped her until she met Jesus. She was bleeding alongside when Jesus was bleeding on His journey to the cross. She bled the same path as Jesus did; being shamed.

The woman bleeding is in comparison to the bleeding wounds of Jesus as He journeyed to and on the cross. The woman is bleeding but what is the cause of her bleeding? As the scripture says, the serpent will bruise the heel of the seed of the woman (Genesis 3:15). This is the bruising of the heel of her offspring by the serpent causing the woman to bleed.

"In the beginning, the Word already existed; the Word was with God, and the Word was God. From the very beginning, the Word was with God. Through him God made all things; not one thing in all creation was made without him."
(John 1:1-3)

As God said in the scriptures, He will bring enmity between the woman and the serpent. This enmity is Jesus Christ, who came and died on the cross to bring us liberty and put an end to the bleeding of the woman. This healing came about when the woman touched the stripes of Jesus. God said to the serpent, *the seed of the woman will crush your head.* This whole journey of Jesus is to bring peace to mankind and birth the new church of peace.

The Night Jesus Shared His Blood on The Cross

The night Jesus shared His blood on the cross is incredible. On the cross, Jesus was nailed both in the hands and feet to it and was pierced in His side, making it five wounds obtained on the cross. He bled on the cross. He brought liberty to us on the cross. We have talked about Jesus' journey to the cross, but on it, Jesus left the body that has been whipped by the crowd to die. On the cross, the Lord is crucified to bring defamation to the kingdom.

He stayed on the cross till all was done, then He fell to His sleep. On the cross, He bought man with His blood and changed man's destiny. That is what Jesus did that night on the cross. He changed the destiny of man. For man to change his destiny, man has to come to the cross to be healed. You cannot go to it without going through Jesus, because He is the master of the cross. He went to it with no blemish on His body. He came to the cross with His mastery in withstanding the lives of man. He is the master of the cross because He came to it single-handedly. He came to the cross with His broken body, and on it, He bled.

On that cross, He took our transgressions and died with them. He bled on the cross for the church. On that rugged cross, Jesus bled, and His blood on it is a symbol of how hard He worked to bring us peace, to bring us out of the bleeding condition that the church is suffering from. The church is in her dying moment and needs the hand of God in bringing her together. The cross as rugged as it looks stands for our salvation. In order to bring us salvation, Jesus bled on that cross. Before Jesus died on that cross, He bled on it; a sign of who He is, the Savior.

The cross stands for who we are and what we are made of; an intersection of human flesh and the Spirit of God. On that intersection, God brought justice to man. He liberated us from the hands of the enemy and placed us in His court. On the cross, that night was the end of our struggle, but to reach that end needs dedication. You cannot go to the cross without dedication and a constant reminder of who you are—a child of God.

God brought the cross to us in the form of Jesus Christ. He created us to be the worship. The cross stands for our liberation and defense. We defend and liberate ourselves with it. The church cannot do without the cross. You cannot remove it from the church; the church becomes meaningless. The church needs the cross to be her head in order to bring her salvation. It stands for our crisis and how they were all defeated by Jesus Christ. It is a reminder of our faith.

We cannot have church without the cross; it is our backbone, our foundation. How can you remove the cross from the church and replace it with something else? It is impossible! That is what the present church is doing; removing the sense of God from the church and replacing it with man.

God needs to be in our churches, and our churches need God, but which God? That is the question. Which God are you placing in your church, the God of life or the God of death (Genesis 2:8-9)? They all come in the same form, how will you know who is who? Until you visit the cross, you will not know who the right God is.

> *Then the Lord God planted a garden in Eden, in the East, and there he put the man he had formed. He made all kinds of beautiful trees grow there and produce good fruit. In the middle of the garden stood the tree that gives life and the tree that gives knowledge of what is good and what is bad.*
> **(Genesis 2:8-9; GNT)**

> *He told him, "You may eat the fruit of any tree in the garden, except the tree that gives knowledge of what is good and what is bad. You must not eat the fruit of that tree; if you do, you will die the same day."*
> **(Genesis 2:16-17)**

In the middle of the Garden of Eden in Genesis 2: 8 through 9, stood the tree of life and the tree of the knowledge of good and evil. This is our cross, the cross that man has to fight to defend. This is the cross that Christ died on by breaking down the desires of the flesh against the will of God. This is our cross; the desires of our heart and the will of God. On that intersection, Christ died to save us from the atrocities of that cross.

Man brought the two wills together the day we gave in to the enemy in Genesis 3 when he failed to stand fast on the word of God. We failed in our duty to believe in Him who planted us in that garden. We failed God, and the two trees became our cross to bear—the tree of life and the tree of death. The tree of death is what we are trying to die to, but the process is tedious. You cannot go to the cross without Jesus.

God did not put us in the garden to bring us death, but He placed us there to bring us life and this life has been taken from us by the serpent. So, how do we claim this life back from the enemy? That is the whole idea of us dying to the flesh and lifting the banner of Christ. Jesus Christ has already set the bar by going to the cross and dying to the flesh. How far will the church go to get healed?

CHAPTER TWO

She Came Up from Behind

She came up in the crowd behind Jesus and touched the edge of his cloak, and her bleeding stopped at once.
(Luke 8:44; GNT)

"Come to me, all of you who are tired from carrying heavy loads and I will give you rest. Take my yoke and put it on you, and learn from me, because I am gentle and humble in spirit; and you will find rest. For the yoke I will give you is easy, and the load I will put on you is light."
(Matthew 11:28–30; GNT)

He gives strength to the weary and increases the power of the weak. Even youths grow tired and weary, and young men stumble and fall; but those who

hope in the Lord will renew their strength. They will soar on wings like eagles; they will run and not grow weary, they will walk and not be faint.
(Isaiah 40:29–31)

Comparing the texts of Luke 8:42 and 13:11-13, Jesus did not call to the woman with the issue of blood to heal her. It was the woman who reached out to Jesus for healing. Jesus did not place His hands on her, but it was the woman who touched the hem of Jesus' garment for healing. For she said to herself, "If only I may touch His garment, I shall be made well" (Matthew 9:2; NKJV). The difference here is the act of reaching out to God or God reaching out to you.

On the back of Jesus are the stripes of His sufferings; therefore, the woman's reason for approaching Jesus from behind because of what she has heard about Him. On the back of Jesus is her healing. She touched the presence of God by visiting the Lord's chamber. She has learned about the Son of God and what He represents. She has learned about all the miracles He has performed and the mystery that follows Him.

He is the Son of God and mystery comes with Him. She brought herself to understand who God is in the midst of His people. The woman has heard about Jesus, the Wonderful Counsellor, the Mighty God, the Eternal Father, the Savior, the Healer, the Prince of Peace, and the Restorer. She has heard about all the things He does. If she has to identify with Jesus to heal her, then she has to reach Him in the right place.

The woman has searched everywhere for help for her condition; from one doctor to another but to no avail. The woman has searched through the land for her healing, but healing came from nowhere. She has spent all her money on doctors for treatment, instead of being healed, her condition grew worse (Mark 5:25–27). She has heard about the Lord Jesus Christ but has not seen Him yet. She has been convinced of His healing power but has not been able to reach Him. So, there is a woman desperately seeking for help and heard that the Lord has come to town.

Coming up from Behind

On the back of Jesus are His bleeding wounds and crushing in on Him is the crowd. Wearing on the back of Jesus is the sign of His sufferings for us. The touching of the hem of His garment or cloak is a representation of who Jesus is, the Messiah. He took on the flesh of man and had it broken into pieces that could not be sewn together. This is the reason the woman with the issue of blood touched Jesus' hem for healing.

The woman needs the hem of Jesus' garment to be healed as He integrates into His spiritual self. She needed the hem of the garment in her life to be healed of her condition; so is the need of the word of God in the life of man. The hem is the border to our soul. The Word of God is the border to her soul; so, the woman touched the border to her soul.

The Son of God came in His infinite self to save mankind. The garment Jesus is wearing covers His infinite self and as you touch Him in the right place through His garment—that is, the covering over his actual self of who He is, God—you will be healed. Jesus has all these wounds on His back to be reached by the church for healing in a time of need.

The woman listened to the Word of God and brought healing to her soul. She touched the bleeding wounds for her healing. The blood from the wounds of Jesus exchanged for the blood of the woman. Jesus sacrificed Himself for our peace on earth. The Lord is carrying our salvation on His back. Until the woman touched Jesus' hem, she was bleeding everywhere she went. She met no cure for her condition. But as she touched the hem of Jesus' garment, her bleeding stopped. This explains why God promised the serpent in the Garden of Eden that the seed of the woman will crush the serpent's head and the serpent will bruise her seed's heel (Genesis 3:15). The seed of the woman will one day stop the serpent in his path. The woman has been following Jesus and could not reach out to Him because of the crowd crushing in on Him, but she reached out to Him going against the route of the crowd. She touched the hem of His garment to bring salvation to herself and peace within her.

When the woman touched the hem—it brought Jesus and her together; humanity and divinity—it generated power in the woman. The merging of the two souls created a bond between Jesus and the woman. The creation of that bond brought Jesus to the realization that power has gone out of Him. Binding the soul of man with that of God brings restoration.

Wearing the outer covering is for us to learn who Jesus is in the name of God. The covering is for our purpose, to bring us peace. The covering has Christ in it—the purpose of Christ, but are we touching the hem of His garment? Is Christ in us or are we wandering around looking for Him? We share in His sufferings, so shall we reach Him through His sufferings. We are one with Christ, and as such, we live in Him and Him in us.

The woman with the issue of blood touched the hem of Jesus' garment for her peace. She changed her life around—she shifted in her life. She formed a union with the light of the world. She changed her position as the woman with the issue of blood to the daughter of Jesus. Her position changed.

She Shifted!

The woman reached from the back due to her belief. Her faith led her to the back of Jesus.

The touching of the hem joined two worlds together; the bleeding world and the world that has the cure to the bleeding. The woman touches the part where both worlds joined together, that is, Jesus, who is the humanity of God on earth. She touched the combination of man and God, and that represent the hem—where God starts and when man ends. This is a combination of His love for us. God has given Christ to us as a solution to our problem of divinity. He has been given to help us live the life God has ordained for mankind.

The whole concept is about God bringing us together to the level of Christ—shaming the enemy and lifting us above our limitations. God created the world for it to know who He is in the end. In the end, He united both worlds. The wounds on Jesus' back are a representation of who He is—our Deliverer. He came on earth only to save man from the hands of the enemy. Jesus brought man peace in His heart. The woman touched the very soul of God, Jesus; for this reason, Jesus felt power go out of Him.

She touched Him!

The woman touched the hem of Jesus' garment.

The Hem

- (Definition) An edge or border on a piece of cloth, especially a finished edge, as for a garment or curtain, made by folding an edge under and stitching it down.

In the Bible,

> *"The LORD commanded Moses to say to the people of Israel: "Make tassels on the corners of your garments and put a blue cord on each tassel. You are to do this for all time to come. The tassels will serve as reminders, and each time you see them you will remember all my commands and obey them; then you will not turn away from me and follow your own wish-*

es and desires. The tassels will remind you to keep all my commands, and you will belong completely to me. I am the LORD your God; I brought you out of Egypt to be your God. I am the LORD."
(Numbers 15:37–41)

The Lamb of God was slain for the benefit of man.

Question: **How do you know who Jesus Christ is?**
Answer: He is the lamb with the bleeding wounds on His back.

Question: **How do you approach Jesus from behind?**
Answer: You study the Scriptures diligently because you think that in them you have eternal life. These are the very Scriptures that testify about me, yet you refuse to come to me to have life.
(John 5:39-40; NIV)

Question: **How did the woman touch Jesus?**
Answer: By touching the very soul of Christ.

You have heard about Jesus, but how will you identify Him when you come across many who claim to be Him? Jesus Christ is the One with marks of suffering on His back. He is the one wearing the bleeding wounds of His suffering on His back. The

Old Testament prophesied about Jesus bringing healing to the sick (Isaiah 35:5–6). The woman has heard about Jesus, but who is He?

Grabbing onto the Power

The question is, "How do you grab onto the power that heals?"

Here comes Jesus in His priestly garment walking around doing His Father's work (Luke 6:16-21), but how do you touch this garment on Him as He walks with the crowd? He is wearing this garment opposed to His royal apparel. God has taken off His royal garment and taken upon Himself the nature of man; flesh. God took on the garment of servanthood; coming to us in the flesh as Immanuel. How is it possible to draw any power from this servanthood garment?

The woman touched the servanthood garment by wearing the same garment as Jesus. She remembered Numbers 15:37-41. Seeing the hem of Jesus' garment reminded her of all commands of God and touched the garment by obeying them. The woman is wearing the same garment as Jesus, but the only difference is, Jesus is born of the Spirit. His inner man is the Spirit of God. Although the Lord has been annointed to be our Savior, He has to come to us in humility.

The woman had to reach Him, and the only way to do so is by accessing Him through His outer garment. He wears the nature of man on Him, but He is of God and has the Spirit of

God in Him. The hem is the boundary between His human nature and His divine nature.

Luke 9:1 and Luke 10:19 says Jesus has given power and authority to His disciples to walk on snakes, drive out all demons, and heal the sick. We just need a constant reminder of the power and authority that we exert. The woman is going through this struggle of how to establish herself but does not remember that she possesses this power and authority that can eradicate every misery she is going through. Dedication is the first weapon to poverty. You cannot be poor if you are dedicated to your cause. The question is, how do you become dedicated to your cause? To be dedicated to your cause, you must have faith in what you do or believe. You must stay true to your faith. You cannot change your cause if you are dedicated to Jesus Christ.

The woman came behind from the crowd to touch the hem of Jesus' garment. It is a good sign because she has found where she belongs and to do so, she had to come into terms with her situation and devise a plan on how to touch His garment. She came behind from the crowd to touch Jesus; she took a decisive thought. She brought down the barriers that were deceiving her from going close to Jesus. She rendered herself vulnerable to the Lord and made her case to Him, and the Lord heard her prayer and granted her healing. We possess this power of healing. All we have to do is to reach out the Jesus in our dying need and ask for forgiveness, and He shall grant us peace.

In our dying need, we must seek the face of God. We must reach out to Jesus; touch the hem of His garment and pray for forgiveness. That is all!

We Must Touch the Hem of His Garment!

How do you feel the garment of the Lord?

-    By touching it

How do you change your garment to His?

-    By taking His word

God loves us no matter what we do, but to get us to understand who Christ is, is difficult. You cannot teach someone Jesus, but you can show someone who He is. All that we do is to show who Jesus is to the crowd around Him. Teaching who Jesus Christ is to man is difficult, but Jesus works on our hearts in believing in Him. He teaches our heart who He is and works on our belief. How do we believe in Him when all our thought about Him is judgment? We do not talk about Him as the friendly God He is but as a dictator.

The Woman and the Cross She Fell in Love With

The cross the woman fell in love with is the mystery behind the touching of the hem of Jesus' garment. She fell in love with the cross that God places on earth by defending the faith of Jesus Christ. The woman who fell in love with God also fell in love with His Son, Jesus Christ. She brought the church closer to God. We now know that Jesus is in God and God is in Him (John 14:9; John 1:14; Colossians 1:15). The woman covered herself with the garment but touched only the hem of the garment to prove love to the nation.

Just as I was meditating on this, I had an epiphany that the full covering of a woman in garment is not for the benefit of the church but the obedience of the church. The covering of a woman is not mandatory but only for the woman to remember what Jesus Christ did for her. It is for the need of the woman. God covered Adam and Eve with garments of animal skins (Genesis 3: 7-12; 21). He gave Adam and Eve garments to cover their nakedness.

God put some principles in place of our sin. These principles cover our mistakes and put us right with God, so when God sees us, He does not see our faults but sees the covering He has placed on us. That covering is Jesus. These garments are the garment of faith in Jesus Christ. God gave the man the principles of life. You cannot live life without having His principles, and this is what Jesus Christ came on earth to teach us—to place back the love that God has for us.

We killed that love in us when man fell for the lies of the serpent. The reason for the garment of skins is to fetch the church from her grave, and not for man gender to impose this nature on the woman. God gave man the opportunity to dig himself out of the grave. The garment on the woman is to cover her nakedness and not bring shame to the church. The act is for the church and not man. This act was not given to man to oppose women. The woman stands for the church, and the act of recovery from the hands of the enemy is the duty of the church.

Many people are surrounding Jesus but not touching His earthly nature. The church is touching the nature of Jesus they are used to; His heavenly being without going through His earthly being. You need Jesus Christ in all things pertaining to life. Yes, the crowd is surrounding Jesus and crushing in on Him but which nature of Him are they crushing in on; His earthly or heavenly nature? There are two sides to Him, which one are you trying to reach?

You cannot go to the cross without going through Jesus Christ; He is the cross. He is the suffering. He is the tribulations. He is the light. He is your salvation. You need to go through Him to get to the Heavenly Father. He is the way, the truth, and the life (John 14:6).

The woman fell in love with the garment; the covering on Jesus. She knew the purpose of it, touched it, and immediately was healed. She has been following Jesus from afar, but as she got closer to Him, she found love and peace in Him. She fell in love with Jesus and the covering He had on.

Without that covering, Jesus will not be who He is, the image of God on earth—Immanuel. Jesus is the representation of the three persons of the Godhead on earth; the Father, the Son, and the Holy Spirit. This is how the woman saw Jesus as, representing who the Father is. The woman fell in love with the Most High God, but to reach the Father, she had to go through His Son, Jesus Christ.

For God to come to our aid, He has to present Himself as man in our time. And to do so, God had to birth Himself to us as Jesus Christ; the Most High God in the flesh of man to exist in time because He is eternal. His reason for calling Jesus, the High Priest, is because Jesus is a representation of Him on earth. Jesus has brought us good news on earth. God birthed Himself to man before He could help man and He did that through Jesus Christ, His Son. You cannot birth yourself unless you know who you are birthing it to. God brought the church in heaven to earth for us to replicate His church on earth. In other words, we have to wear the church on us on earth to change our definition of what church is. God brought to man on earth His will (Matthew 6:10–13).

When man sinned against God in the Garden of Eden, man was sent out of the garden and made to cultivate the soil from which they have been formed from. In other words, man was sent out of the garden to work on his human nature; the flesh. The entire struggle we are going through is to overcome our fleshly lust and make God our desire. We are to work on our nature for it to be fruitful to us (Genesis 3:17–19). This garden is then protected from man.

God birth His Son to us to bring the lost church back to Him. His Son wears the nature of man (the flesh, the outer covering) and God (the inner man). With His covering on, the woman had to touch it to get closer to the Father, because the covering is who Jesus is. God took on the body of man, and it is with this body that He came to earth, and it is through this body that you will find your salvation. You cannot get to God without going through His Son. He is the partition in the Holy of Holies in the tabernacle (Exodus 36) that tore from the top to the bottom.

Above all the things in the Holy Place, you cannot go to the Holy of Holies without going through the partition. Jesus Christ is the partition, and He tore it down. He broke the silence between God and man. He is the way to the Father. He is the bridge between God and man and He is the enmity between the serpent and the woman.

For the woman to get to God, she has to fall in love with the garment (Exodus 39:1–30) on Jesus. She fell in love with Jesus Christ, the Savior of this world and brought peace to the church. The woman changed her desire for that of the church. She gave all her worship to Jesus Christ. She changed her life around for the love of God. She shifted! She succeeded in herself and brought salvation to the church. She elevated the church from where she was to that of Christ and let the church lead in the war of strive.

The church will strive forever until the day comes when man will strive no more. That will be the end of time when the church will choose Christ as her head. That time will come soon! The woman fell in love with the church that is to replace who she is. The church that the woman fell in love with was a church of faith. Her faith is tied to Jesus Christ. The toast of the woman is the church of today! They slave for no one.

Subject to Belief

The woman had faith in God and believed in His Son, Jesus Christ. She trusted in Jesus as her Savior. Therefore, He brought salvation to her. It all ends up in "belief." The belief she had for Jesus brought healing to her instantly. It takes the heart of man to believe in Christ. If you do not have the heart of Christ, you will not believe in Him. It takes consecration to build your faith in Christ. It does not take a day but takes centuries to build the kind of faith the woman had in Jesus. She wandered around the earth seeking for healing, but healing never came to her until she learned about the word of God. This brought restoration to her and the people around her. She changed the lives of people because of her faith in the word of God.

According to the word of God, all things are possible for those who believe in Him and come to Him (Matthew 19:23–30). He has prepared a place for us that one day we will all inherit. Do not assume that God does not love you. He loves all. No assumptions that Jesus Christ does not exist because He does in your mind. God created us based on His word, and it is through His word that we live. If His word lives, so do Jesus in our hearts. He prays for us every day that we live to understand the word of God in our hearts.

The LORD said to the woman in the Book of Genesis 3:16, "I will increase your trouble in pregnancy and your pain in giving birth. In spite of this, you will still have a desire for your husband, yet you will be subject to him." The church will be the subject of faith. Man will believe in His Creator. We will live by His word and walk by His word.

CHAPTER THREE

Who Touched Me?

> *Jesus asked, "Who touched me?"*
> *Everyone denied it, and Peter said, "Master, the peo-*
> *ple are all around you and crowding in on you."*
> *But Jesus said, "Someone touched me, for I knew it*
> *when power went out of me."*
> (Luke 8:45-46)

So the Lord God sent them out of the Garden
of Eden and made them cultivate the soil from
which they had been formed.
(Genesis 3:23; GNT)

Someone touched Me, Jesus said, *because power has gone out of Me.* "Who touched me?" He asked. This is a powerful statement to make. How can He tell that He has been touched if He was only touched on the hem of His garment? The outer garment has no sensory nerves in it; so, how did He feel this touch? How can Jesus tell power has gone out of Him by just being touched, not on the flesh but His garment? Does that mean He wasn't really touched on a physical outer garment?

The Touch

There was a crowd waiting for Him on the other side of the lake, and when He got there, they crowded in on Him, but none touched him as the woman did. What does that tell us as a church or individual? Are we doing the work of God or our work? We seem to be walking with Him but not touching His garment. Why is our walk with Jesus not feeling like a touch on His garment? We claim to be walking with Him, but are we? The days are getting closer, and Jesus is not feeling our touch. What are we doing as believers in Christ? Are we following Him and not believing in Him? Do we believe in other faiths? What is it that we are doing that does not meet His requirements?

We are definitely not doing something right because when Jesus asked the question, everyone denied touching Him in His garment. When the woman happened to see that she has been found out, she came in humility and fell at Jesus' feet. It talks about ministry and our dedication. The woman fell to Jesus' feet and made her worship known. In the presence of the crowd surrounding Jesus, the woman told them her "why" and "how." She confirmed her faith in Jesus and witnessed the word of God to all. She became the church God promised; with faith in Him and belief in His Son, Jesus Christ. She became the resurrected church of God.

The touching of the garment is a representation of who you are and who God is. The woman touched the hem of Jesus' garment to bring the liberty God spoke about in Genesis chapter 3. Jesus is the link between God and man; He is the bridge. Touching the hem of Jesus' garment is touching the interface of man and God. It is at this interface that man shares his attributes with God, and it is at this same interface that God shares His attributes with man, in a sense, birthing Jesus at this interface. With Jesus on the cross, the interface becomes God's only as the flesh is being killed on the cross. Touching the hem reveals who Jesus is and what He came on earth to do. He came to be our pacifier in the matter of sin and bring us back to God; therefore, His reason for killing the flesh on the cross and resurrecting the spirit on the third day. The woman touched the divinity of Christ and brought healing to her ill body. She healed herself by touching the inner self of Christ which is the Spirit of God.

The church is to bring liberty to the people and liberty comes from God who, in turn, has ushered His Son, Jesus Christ, to come to earth and liberate us from the hands of the enemy. We are in transition to His throne. God has brought us on earth to bring this transition in place. She touched the hem of Jesus' garment to crush the head of the serpent in our life. Someone has to put an end to the enemy's work. Just as Jesus drove the animals and moneychangers from the Temple in Jerusalem, so will He change the destiny of the church. He will bring the seed of the serpent out of the church.

We are linking the church with her destiny. A link was formed between the woman and Jesus, and this link is to bring liberty to the church. What is this link? The chain being formed is from the Lord to the church, the woman with the issue of blood. A chain is formed, and with that chain, no one can penetrate through to break the link and destroy the church. The unification of the Lord with the church will bring unity in the church. That is what the woman did by touching the hem of Jesus' garment; bringing unity to the church. She reached out to Jesus from the awkward place, and this brought out the liberty that the church needs, and with that touch, Jesus asked, *who touched me?* Because He felt power has gone out of Him and into the desired church. He felt the connection between Him and the woman, the perfect connection to be made. He knew the time has come for Him to give the liberty He has been given; so He said in verse 48, *my daughter, your faith has made you well. Go in peace.* He knew the connection had been made and this is the time to proclaim to the church, "Go in peace."

The Power

The Power that transcends from Jesus!

"But Jesus said, someone touched me, for I knew it when power went out of Me." With all the people around Him, none of them admitted touching the Lord Jesus.

In Jesus is light; light is energy and light shines in darkened places: as the woman places her hand on His garment, the light in Him shone on the woman and this produced energy in her and energy out of Him. Power is the amount of energy transferred over time. We live in darkened places. But because He had this power in Him, He felt the touch because the woman had nothing in her. She lacked in the places that Jesus filled with His power.

The woman touched Jesus in a place that no one has ever touched, in His innermost self for Him to feel power go out of Him. What is then the link between the woman and the hem of Jesus' garment as power went out of Jesus when she touched Him? Power was transferred from His garment to the woman.

God, in the Book of Genesis Chapter 3 said: *The seed of the woman will crush the serpent's head.* What do you need to crush the serpent's head? Power and where is this power? It is in Jesus. Jesus has been given the authority from God to crush the head of the serpent. Therefore, the only way to get healed from this bleeding is through Jesus Christ, the Son of God.

The power Jesus has is in the cords He knotted together to form the whip in Mark 11:15-17. His power is centered in the cords of the whip. In the whip is the power to crush the head of the serpent and in the whip is the authority Jesus has to bring the church down and resurrect her in three days. In all these is His power to heal the woman with the issue of blood.

The power consists of His nature as man and God, and with His human nature, He crushed the head of the serpent; there is His reason for dying on the cross for sin. And with divine nature, He brought the church down and raised her on the third day. This is the power He holds, and every man has to touch this power to eradicate every sickness in their body.

The power of God is centered in us and to enable it, we must meet God in His infinite self as Jehovah—the provider of our life. To be healed of your illness, you must touch the hem of Jesus' garment to seek His face. You must tie the cords around you to feel the power of Jesus on you. Power went out of Him because He is power; the authority that you and I have over the serpent.

A Whip Out of Cords

Jesus made a whip out of cords. He brought the cords together as one and drove out the animals and moneychangers in the Temple with it. He changed the destiny of the church by bringing together the cords of the Word—His Omniscience, Omnipotence, Omnipresence, and the cord of man. Jesus brought together all these three attributes of God and man to drive the enemy out of the church. Jesus showed the enemy who He, Jesus is.

How did He do the whipping? God, in the Book of Genesis chapter eight, says in His heart that He will not bring calamity on earth again (Genesis 8:20–22). So, how is He going to bring liberty to the church? He has planned to save the church, but how?

Jesus brought calmness to the church, but the church was not at peace until Jesus brought her peace. He did all these by going to the cross. You cannot go to the cross without passing through the church. You need to see the state of the church to bring her peace. Jesus brought this peace by going to Calvary. Without His journey to Calvary, we would not have this peace that we cry for. You cannot see Christ without seeing the cross.

Jesus is the cross; He brought humanity and divinity together to bring this salvation. The knotting of humanity and divinity brought the cords together to form the whip. So, without humanity, the cords wouldn't have formed and so is without divinity. You need both to form the cords that Jesus made into a whip. It is all in the plan. Bringing both surfaces together created the interface that the woman touched on Jesus' garment. It was through Him that the cross was made.

You cannot exchange your life for that of Christ without visiting the cross. Everyone must visit the cross. What is stopping the crowd from visiting the cross? The humiliations and sufferings of the cross are beyond them. That is their fear. The church is full of divination but going to the cross is a problem. How is the church going to come out of it? Staying in the church in her current state is lethal.

Why are we fighting over money when the Lord we worship can give us richly all things to enjoy? Why are we fighting over money in the church when we are to inherit His kingdom? We are the inheritors of His kingdom, so why the envy over money? Jesus chattered their coins, and this brought unity to the church. Bringing out the moneychangers brings unity in the church. The church becomes one and unified.

The sufferings of the church are going to be lethal. In Isaiah chapter seven, it says when that time comes, God "will hire a barber from across the Euphrates—the emperor of Assyria! —and he will shave off your beards and the hair on your heads and your bodies" (Isaiah 7:20; GNT). He will bring salvation to us. God will bring in the sufferings. That is why you will have to teach your child according to the word of God; this is crucial. The church will be in trouble in the hands of God. That is when He will separate the wheat from the weeds; differentiate who you are and who I am, all through His word. God is here on earth with us, Immanuel, but can you tell Him from the crowd?

God is bringing the barber from across the Euphrates to earth, and as he approaches the earth, things are going to change for good. He will bring peace to it and change its destiny.

Healing the Woman

When they arrived in Jerusalem, Jesus went to the Temple and began to drive out all those who were buying and selling. He overturned the tables of the moneychangers and the stools of those who sold pigeons, and he would not let anyone carry anything through the Temple courtyards. He then taught the people: "It is written in the Scriptures that God said, 'My Temple will be called a house of prayer for the people of all nations.' But you have turned it

into a hideout for thieves!"
(**Mark 11:15–17**)

Inside the sanctuary of God are the moneychangers, the pigeon-sellers, buyers, and sellers. First, Jesus drove out the animals, both the sheep and the cattle and then overturned the tables of the moneychangers and scattered their coins. He then ordered the pigeon sellers to take them out. They are occupying the sanctuary of God which is meant to be called a house of prayer for the people of all nations. This sanctuary has been turned into a hideout of thieves, what does that say to us in this now-church? It tells us that the church is a place where everything has to be laid down as profit-ridden.

Around Jesus is the crowd surrounding Him. Around Him is the crowd waiting to see who Jesus is, explore Him to find out who He is, what is in Him, what He is made of, is He originally from God or a figment of the imagination of the church? These are the crowd waiting to see Jesus on the other side of the lake when He got there. They were almost crushing in on Him because He is from God and God is the ultimate solution to their problem, but who is God if I may ask?

He is the sovereign ruler of the universe. We worship Him because He is the God of all creation and man is indebted to Him. Jesus came from God, and as such, man has to find out exactly who He is in the kingdom. Man has searched everywhere for His destiny, but the destiny of man does not come with ease. It comes with dedication and adoration.

Searching for God in different places will not help you because the God we are searching for is in Jesus Christ, the Deliverer. So, searching for God in different places brings you back to the same place—the cross of Jesus. You cannot find Jesus without the cross, and you cannot locate God without going through the cross. The work of the disciples is to bring you to the cross of Jesus, not to bring you to destruction; that is what the church is doing now.

Eliminating the word of the LORD from the church and replacing it with the word of the world. They are exchanging the will of the church for the will of the world. They teach doctrines that are not meant to be in the church but outside the church. That is why when Jesus asked who touched Him, they all denied it because they have been teaching outside His court (outer court of the tabernacle) and not inside His court, (Holy Place of the tabernacle). They have all been exchanging these vulnerable people for the word of the world. They are selling the destinies of the individuals in the church to the world. They have changed their understanding of the word of God for that of the world. Therefore, the reason for them almost crushing in on Him but not touching His garment. They are closer to Jesus but are not intimately close to Him. They have seen Jesus but do not know Him.

The church is playing with the soul of man and discarded all her principles because of money and fame, but all these will one day fade away and what will the church do because it is written in the Bible that "all things will pass away, but the word of the Lord will remain" (Matthew 24:35; 1 John 2:17)? That is the word from the Lord. He will always remain with us but the works of the devil will one day pass away and who will you be left with? Teach the word of God to the church as they need it for their development and growth. The church will always be here teaching the word of God but make sure you teach the un-adulterated word of God; the word that has not been tampered with. We are all God's children.

So, what is the church doing, now that the word of God is with us? How are they treating the word? We go to church every day, but depending on who your pastor or leader is, is the word of God always ministered to you? Is it by word of the minister or by the word of God because there is a thin line between the truth and the exaggerated truth (lie)?

Jesus came to the church to bring us light, but is the light reflecting in our lives? If it is not reflecting in our lives, then there is something wrong with that light. Jesus is saying follow Me as your director, and I will show you the land flowing with milk and honey, but if you do not follow Me, then you will end up in the land full of destruction. God is not destroying you, but you are destroying yourself from being healed. It is the land that God blessed and cursed at the same time. You can be healed in that land or be cursed in that same land depending on how you see God. Bringing restoration to yourself is your purpose, and you should approach it cautiously with the word of God in mind.

The church is there for our healing, but we are being deceived by the very people who hold our healing in their hands—the leaders of the church. They are capitalizing on our healing and exchanging them for gifts. The church is to heal people, but they are selling or trafficking the people under their authority.

They are dealing the faith of these people for their own benefits. Teach the word of God in the church, and it shall be well with the church. Teaching your own word yields nothing but destruction. The church is in the phase of being birth again. Everything in the church has changed due to our greediness and disrespect.

We sell our souls to the church and they, in turn, feed us with lies about the word of God. They change our attitude toward God. If the sanctuary of God will be called the house of prayer for the people of all nations, what is it been called now? Strange, we all call it the house of God. Is it really His house? As the text says, it has turned into the hideout of thieves.

Are we really worshipping God, and if we are, does it fit the description God has given it? *His sanctuary will be called*, that means it hasn't reached the qualification yet, and we are still calling it the Lord's sanctuary. The Lord is preparing a place for His sanctuary, and that place will be called a house of prayer for the people of all nations. Do you classify your church as such? Look into your church and see if it fits the category?

The churches we have built, have been built upon false promises and the Lord is here to fix those promises. That is why the church has to die and resurrect in order to receive the blessing God has placed on her. The Body of Christ has to be torn down and rebuild in order to save the church. He broke the body up into pieces and rebuild (put it together) it into the perfect shape. Jesus brought the body under stress, tore the body up, and sewed it together in perfect shape. The body of Jesus Christ underwent extreme torture by being whipped; the very whip He made out of cords to cleanse the Temple in Jerusalem.

He cleansed the sanctuary of God by His whip. He divided the sanctuary and brought division among them and with that division, He births unity among the church. Starting from the top, He drove out those who were buying and selling in the sanctuary with His whip, overturned their fixtures (tables and stools) and stopped anyone carrying anything through the temple courtyard. This tells you how deviated we are from the word of God. If God can come down in His human form to liberate us from this treacherous behavior, then there is a problem with the church today.

Jesus did not only drive the buyers and sellers out of the church; He also taught them the word of God; the truth of God's word. The light that is to bring them out of the darkness; making sure the wisdom imparted on the church stops any false doctrine entering her gates.

The church is being fooled by the people who control her, but the Lord will bring His whip made out of cords into the churches to cleanse them of deception. Isaiah 7:20 says, *you will be left exposed and shamed for your evil deeds.* He will bring the church to her lowest form, and we will call her the church of

God. The church will resurrect from her faults. Be careful, the moneychangers in the church. Your time is up. Soon, the Lord will come for His church, and where will you be? The scripture says:

> *"But if it's by God's power that I am sending the evil spirits packing, then God's kingdom is here for sure. How in the world do you think it's possible in broad daylight to enter the house of an awake, able-bodied man and walk off with his possessions unless you tie him up first? Tie him up, though, and you can clean him out. "This is war, and there is no neutral ground. If you're not on my side, you're the enemy; if you're not helping, you're making things worse. "There's nothing done or said that can't be forgiven. But if you deliberately persist in your slanders against God's Spirit, you are repudiating the very One who forgives. If you reject the Son of Man out of some misunderstanding, the Holy Spirit can forgive you, but when you reject the Holy Spirit, you're sawing off the branch on which you're sitting, severing by your own perversity all connection with the One who forgives."*
> (Matthew 12:29–32; MSG)

The Lord will bring salvation to the church. Would it be too late for you by then? No, because God has planned everything in the church. Unknowingly committing sin is forgivable, but knowingly undermining the will of God is a sin indeed, and the church will be cleansed of such. The church will be cleansed of her unfaithful laborers to bring her unity. She will be called the house of prayer for all people of the nations. This is what the church is to become—a land flowing with milk and honey (Exodus 3:17).

To bring together the healing that you need in your body; you will need to be one with God. Formation of this oneness with God is achieved by the touching of the wounds on Jesus' back.

CHAPTER FOUR
My Daughter!

> *"Jesus said to her, "My daughter, your faith has made you well. Go in peace."*
> **(Luke 8:48)**

Why would Jesus refer to the woman with the issue of blood as "My daughter"?

In the Book of Genesis, we read about the disobedience of man against God's will in the Garden of Eden and how God pronounces judgment on the serpent and the woman in Genesis chapter 3 verse 14 through 16. God then gave liberty to man through the same statement made. This is common knowledge in the Bible (Genesis 3:1–24).

To the Serpent, God pronounced (comparing two different versions of the Bible):

The Good News Bibles says,

"I will make you and the woman <u>hate</u> each other; her offspring and yours will always be enemies. Her offspring will crush your head, and you will bite her offspring's heel."
(Genesis 3:15 - Emphasis added)

The New King James Version says,

"And I will put <u>enmity</u> between you and the woman, and between your seed and her Seed; He shall bruise your head, and you shall bruise His heel."
(Genesis 3:15 – Emphasis added)

To the woman (Church), God pronounced:
The Good News Bible says,

"And he said to the woman, "I will increase your trouble in pregnancy and your pain in giving birth. In spite of this, you will still have desire for your husband, yet you will be subject to him."
(Genesis 3:16)

The New King James Version says,

"To the woman He said: "I will greatly multiply your sorrow and your conception; in pain

*you shall bring forth children; your desire shall
be for your husband, and he shall rule over
you."*
(Genesis 3:16)

*"Adam named his wife Eve, because she was
the mother of all human beings. And the Lord
God made clothes out of animal skins for
Adam and his wife, and he clothed them."*
(Genesis 3:20–21; GNT)

Desire - Powerful word! Your desire shall be for your husband, what a profound statement!? What shall that desire be? Desire as a noun defines as:

- the feeling that accompanies an unsatisfied state
- an inclination to want things

After going through great sorrow in pregnancy and pain in childbirth, the desire of the woman will still be for her husband. She will be subject to him. What a phrase? In pregnancy and childbirth, God says He will greatly increase the pain and sorrow of the woman, but upon all these sorrow and pain, her desire will still be for her husband.

God will bring you to the point that your desire will still be for Him. What is He going to bring into your life that will still make you thirst for Him? God is great because He has set up all these in the name of Jesus. The woman will thirst for the husband through Jesus; therefore, the reason for woman touching the hem of Jesus' garment. God has brought man to a place that man's only desire is to please God and Him alone. That is strange because He gave us everything that we needed in the Garden of Eden, but we still betrayed Him in the garden. So, He decided to take the very thing that fills us up from the garden; His presence, and without His presence, we lack.

God took us from the garden of all supplies and brought us to a place where we will lack, and the only way of fulfilling our need is to look for Him. The Garden of Eden was not a place to empower us, but a place to bring us to His feet as the Lord Jesus Christ. He did not bring us out to fail, but He brought us out to bring us to Himself. That is the logic of the statement. You cannot love God without knowing Him. So, He has to bring you to the stage for you to know Him and love Him deeply.

The desire of the woman will be for her husband, and she will be subject to him. That is a powerful statement because not being subject to him brings different controversies. She will lack so much that she will start looking for other faces to be fulfilled but the Lord brought her to only one place, His side and on His side all things are possible. He will rule over her because He fulfills her needs. Although she has gone through the land looking for help with no success, she found solace in Jesus.

The need that God took from her is peace. The pain that God inflicted on her brings her back to Him; that is the touching of the hem—divine manifestation. She loves Him, and He loves her—the combination of love brings unity and peace. *"My daughter," your faith has made you well. Go in peace*—the restoration word, "peace." There is no restoration without the word "peace." Restoration comes with the word "peace." Jesus in John 14:27 when comforting His disciples said to them, "Peace I leave with you; my peace I give you. I do not give to you as the world gives. Do not let your hearts be troubled and do not be afraid" (GNT).

Three Parts

- The birth of Christ
- The Cross
- The Resurrection of Christ

Parallel to Luke 8:40–56

- The birth of Jairus' daughter
- The Woman with the issue of blood
- the Awakening of the daughter of Jairus

Parallel to

- The birth of the church
- The Journey of the church
- The Resurrection of the Church

There are three parts to this story that Jesus tells the crowd almost caving in on Him.

Part 1

In part 1, we see the church approaching Jesus for help. In Genesis 3:15, we see the birth of both Jesus Christ and the church-to-come. We also see the birth of the "enmity" between the serpent and the woman and the seed of the woman being spoken by God into existence. This is the birthplace of both Jesus Christ and the church-to-come.

The Birth of Christ + The Birth of Jairus' daughter!

Part 2

Part 2, comes the war waged by God—the crushing of the head of the serpent by the seed of the woman, and the bruising of his heel by the serpent. In part 2, we see the woman with the issue of blood seeking healing from Jesus after walking on earth, moving from one healer to another for healing with no avail. She seeks the face of Jesus for redemption. In this part, we see the church seeking help after a long time suffering from the world.

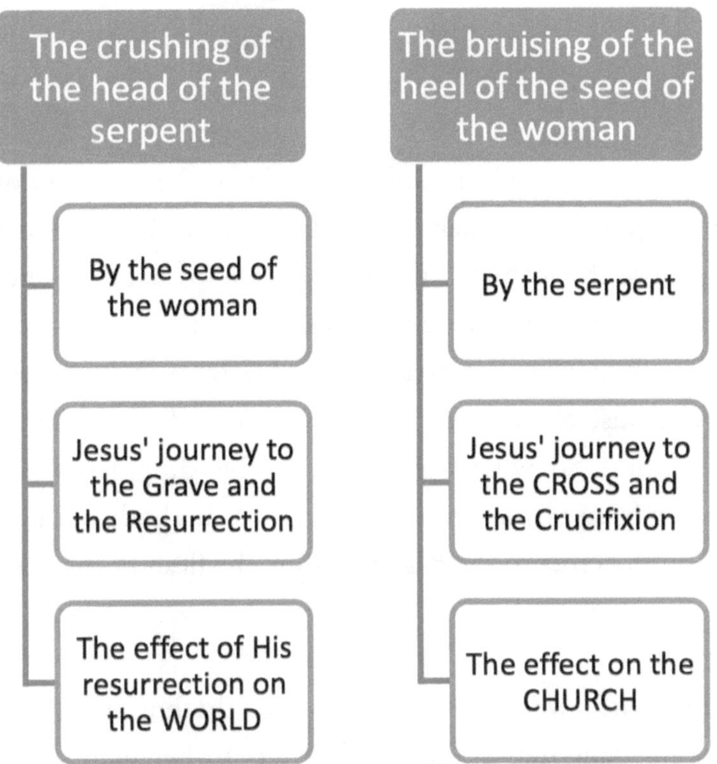

God brought enmity between the serpent and the woman, and the name of the enmity is Jesus Christ. Jesus was born to bring peace to the woman (Mankind).

A child is born to us!
A son is given to us!
And he will be our ruler.
He will be called, "Wonderful Counsellor,"
"Mighty God," "Eternal Father,"

"Prince of Peace."
(Isaiah 9:6)

The enmity God pronounced spoke to the very soul of the woman. Jesus came when the woman was bleeding and took on the pain of the woman—the garment He wore. He suffered on earth for the garment He took on, which is the flesh of man. Jesus took on the character of man. He went through tribulations because of the body He was wearing. He faced the wrath of the world. So, when the woman was bleeding, Jesus was also bleeding from His wounds. He then took this body to the cross, died on the cross to the flesh and took the flesh to the grave.

Part 3

In part 3, we see Jesus traveling to the house of Jairus to bring his daughter to life, as He refers to her inability to respond to any stimuli as a resting phase (sleep). When Jesus died and was buried, He arose on the third day. His resurrection brought power to mankind; therefore, the reason the woman with the issue of blood had to touch His garment in order to be healed. Because in that garment is the redemption power. During His death, burial and resurrection, Jesus overcame the power of death and gained the power of resurrection. Jesus gained the power to resurrect the church. He won over the serpent by crushing its head.

In Luke 8, we see Jesus going into the house of Jairus and clearing every negative thought out of the house, leaving Himself, James, John, Peter, the mother and father of the girl. He changed the atmosphere of the house and called out Jairus' daughter to come forward. He awoke her from her sleep and established His kingdom without negative thoughts but with sincere fellowship.

Jesus broke the curse on the church and released her into her kingship. In the grave, Jesus crushed the head of the serpent by bringing salvation to the church. This is what is going to happen in the future to the church. Resurrection will come to the church. We will see the light, and we will come to the light.

It Is All A Process!

The RESURRECTION of Jesus → The AWAKENING of the Church!

Shared Power!

In this text is a 3-part series of God presenting the church to the crowd. There is a child of age twelve, who is being shown to us as Jairus' daughter. Her father, a man of valor, came looking for healing for the daughter. She is presented to us as a sick child. Jesus then presented the church to us as a woman bleeding for twelve years looking for healing. He then later presented the church to us as Jairus' daughter awakened from her sleep. This is the church in her three stages: 1. bringing the church to birth, 2. aligning the church with the word of God, and 3. bringing the church to fruition.

This is the church we are talking about and the healing of the church through Jesus Christ. Jesus brought peace, healing, and prosperity to the church through His sufferings. Jesus became the pillar between God and man and brought enmity between the church and the serpent. Jesus brought the world out of man. We live in the world but are not of the world. Jesus brought us out to save the church.

This is the stages that the church will go through to bring harmony in the church. So, the bleeding of the woman is the confusion in the church—the division, misunderstanding, complication, manipulations, deceit, etc. The church is bleeding and waiting for God's healing. The church is dying of her illness. This is the journey that the church is on to bring herself to fruition. The church is chasing after many worldly things and leaving the word of God behind. The word of the Lord says He has come to heal the very ground that was cursed. The church is treading on rocky grounds. She is giving all to the world for its benefit. The church that preaches the word of God is left to bleed. The world is taking over the church. The church is being offered to the world.

Question: The world and the church; which are you going for?

In the second phase, you see the church battling with the world, but the world is in favor because it lives in the church. The church has opened her doors to the world to bring its rules and ideas of living in the church. We have a church that is bleeding of love and cannot find love anywhere. She is bleeding of her constitutions and cannot find peace anywhere. And here comes Jesus, the Deliverer, and the church sought help from Him. The church touches His divinity and changed life with herself. The church sought for the face of God after her transgressions.

The Transgressions

The church changed her policies for that of the world. She brought the world into herself and allowed it deposit its worldly policies. The church sold her soul to the world.

> *"The woman saw how beautiful the tree was and how good its fruit would be to eat, and she thought how wonderful it would be to become wise. So she took some of the fruit and ate it. Then she gave some to her husband, and he also ate it. As soon as they had eaten it, they were given understanding and realized that they were naked; so they sewed fig leaves together and covered themselves."*
> **(Genesis 3:6–7; GNT)**

> *"No one can break into a strong man's house and take away his belongings unless he first ties up the strong man; then he can plunder his house."*
> **(Mark 3:27; GNT)**

The Garden of Eden is a place of leverage. We come here because we are in need, and we come here because the Lord is listening to our cry. You do not come to the Garden of Eden if you have all and not in need of help. That is why the Lord said He placed in the garden everything that man needed and nothing less (Genesis 2:4-25).

He created the Garden of Eden to be a place of refuge, but this place has become a place of toil. We live in the garden but do not own anything in the garden. Everything in the garden is for the Lord, and nothing is ours. So, if we are preaching the word of God, we should state how we changed the policy of the garden to ours when we own nothing in there.

We should simplify the way we talk about the garden. We make it sound as if we are the owner of the garden, but we are not. These are the principles God is talking about. Changing the principles of the church does not make any difference as the church is not ours, but the Lord's. Estimating how God will react to your actions is really silly because He does not react to man but His word.

Once God has spoken, so shall it be. This is then a silly question because, how do you tell when God is angry with you because He never changes His mood? He is always with us regardless of what our goal is. He is with us even if we fail Him. He never turns His back on us, so why should you say the Lord is not with us when He is with us?

The changes in the church are massively extensive and need proper structuring; if not, we will lose everything we have in

Jesus' name. We will lose our dignity and prosperity. We will give all to the enemy. As we speak now, the church is in a place of giving everything she has to the world. Our pride has been bought. Our place in the church has changed according to the world. We have placed ourselves in the position of servants and making the servants ride on horsebacks (Ecclesiastes 10:7). This is our situation, but all these will change soon, you will see. The Lord will reverse the process.

The princes will ride the horsebacks, and the servants will walk the earth. We have given so much to the world, and now they are walking over us, but this will stop one day. The church will defeat the world, and the principles of the church will change. The enemy is all over the church; they are everywhere, talking to our children, prophesying to our children and pronouncing a curse on them. When are these going to stop?

We are blind. We cannot see what is going on in the church today. We are lost in our world that we cannot see what is beyond us. The church is failing drastically, and we cannot see. The church is failing her people, and we cannot see. What are we to do to bring this failure out of the church? We are too much into ourselves that we forget the creator of our life; the reason for our existence. We are too much into what we have done that we forget the Lord made us achieve them. We are self-righteous and do not know what we are doing.

The church is failing in the world. The church is failing at everything she does. The church does not sit back to reassess herself to see where the error is coming from. They are all into themselves and not God. They are self-righteous. The changes in the church are ridiculous but who dare point it out as the church is in her millennial stage. Everything has to be millennial and modern for the church to survive, but we forget about the stages of life.

In life, we move from one stage to another. We do not move to a stage without completing the previous phase. Life comes with stages, so does the church. You cannot move from one revolution to another without finishing the former. It has a complete cycle before you move on, but nowadays, man is going beyond its limits. He is proposing things that do not exist in his life and expecting it to happen. That is the problem with the world, and the church has bought it.

It is creating things that do not exist in its creation and making it happen. In such cases, all those things happen through divination (you create to happen when it does not exist in your time). That is the reason I said you should remain in your seat and not sit in the seat of the mockery. You should always be in line with God's word and believe in Him as your Savior. He knows the best. He knows the times and seasons of your life. Do not overlook the work of God. He is working in your favor; wait patiently, it will all come to pass.

The church is the mystery in all these. It is the place where we all meet to pray out to the Lord, and it is the place where all sacrifices are offered. So, you see, you cannot tell a church from the outer court of the tabernacle where mercy is given to people for their wrongdoings.

The church is a place where pardon is given to people. She brings restoration to people and at the same time, gives them peace. But for them to move on to their peaceful place, they have to let go of some things which the church is not willing to do. That is our problem; letting go of the world is our problem, and our soul is attached to this world's system that any persecution that we face, we leverage it with our problems, so we cannot move on to the Holy of holies, where the divine declaration is made. So, we are stuck in the outer court of the tabernacle. We cannot resurrect ourselves from the court to the Holy place where the word of God resides.

The church is in the ground of her own and not rising to any level to bring peace to herself because she has entangled herself with the laws of this world. That is where her problem is coming from; entangling herself with the world for her peace.

The resurrection of the word will bring peace to the church. You cannot change the policies of the church. It must stay the same regardless. The peace of the church is within the church!

Until we loosen ourselves from the grip of the world, we will always be in debt to the world. So, the church headed for the healing of Jesus, and discovered love, and turn to follow Jesus. The church chased after the very thing that she was running away from.

"And he said to the woman, "I will increase
your trouble in pregnancy and your pain in
giving birth. In spite of this, you will still have

> *desire for your husband, yet you will be subject*
> *to him."*
> **(Genesis 3: 16; GNT)**

The desires of the church will remain with the LORD. She chases after the heart of God. The Lord brought healing to the church through dedication. The church changed her process to dedication, and this brought her peace. The church changed her ideas to that of the Son of God and turned her direction from that of the crowd almost crushing Jesus to coming from behind to touch the hem of His garment.

The Daughter of Jairus and the Woman

The daughter of Jairus and the woman with the issue of blood are relations. The Daughter of Jairus and the woman bear no name; the woman has walked the land for twelve years with this condition, and her name was not known. The daughter of Jairus is the church-to-come—the seed of the woman who is to bruise the head of the seed of the serpent. The woman who has the issue of blood is the now-church which God is saving from her illness.

The woman walked around with a condition that no doctor could cure. The woman with the issue of blood is the dying church, which will erupt into the church-to-come. As the church-to-come was conceived and birthed, the woman entered into her condition. The birth of the condition of the woman coincides with the birth of the daughter of Jairus. They were both birthed at the same time, and they both share the same faith.

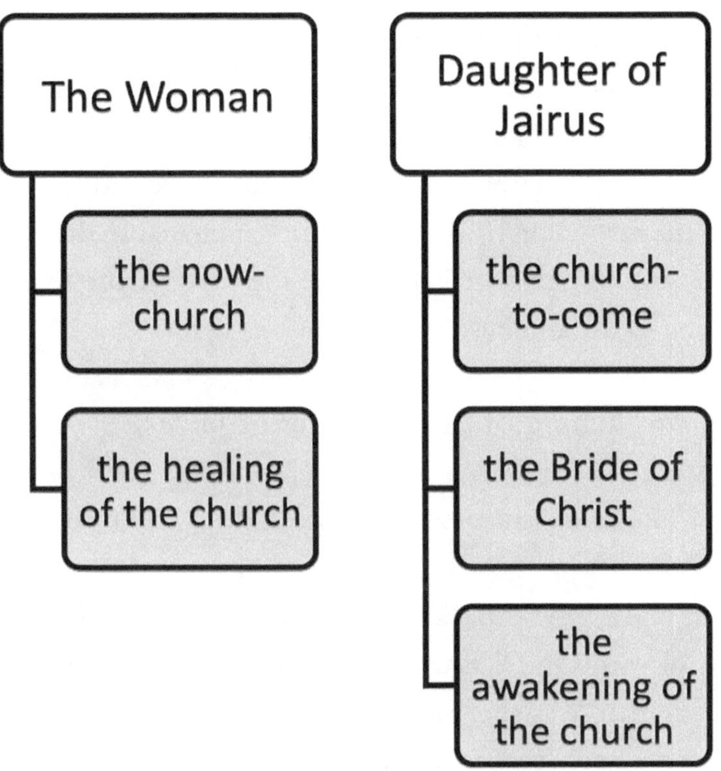

As God in Genesis chapter three pronounces the curse on the woman (church), at the same time, He pronounced her salvation—both were birthed at the same time. As the daughter of Jairus was growing up, the woman was growing in pain with her condition. As the woman in her grows, the daughter in her precedes to her grave. The woman is dying of her illness, and the daughter is dying of strength on her life. Both are dying of the very thing that is to save them; love. They are missing love in their lives, so God brought them together.

Just as the daughter of Jairus was dying, the woman with the issue of blood was getting healed—all in one body; brokenness and wholeness. The daughter is breaking while the woman is making whole, all at the same time—twelve years. Their destinies are being brought together: the church-to-be merged with the now-church. The now-church migrated to the church-to-be; the church that is to bruise the head of the serpent is coming to life and her time is now.

The Awakening of the Daughter of Jairus

Mark 5:41 (ESV) says "Taking her by the hand he said to her, "Talitha cumi," which means, "Little girl, I say to you, arise."

In Luke 8:51–56, when Jesus arrived at the house, He went in with ONLY Peter, James, John, and the child's father and mother. Was the name of the child's mother mentioned in the passage? Jesus was still speaking to the woman in Luke 8:48 when a messenger came to pronounce the death of Jairus' daughter. Just as the woman with the issue of blood was healed of her condition, the daughter of Jairus dies of her illness.

When Jesus got to the home (the church) of Jairus, He saw confusion and heard loud cries and wailing over the death of the girl. He went in and asked them the reason for the confusion, as the girl is only sleeping and not dead. That is what we think about the church today. Everything in the church is dead, and nothing is working within the church. She has lost her strength. But the church (people) started to mock Him, and He put them out of the church (Mark 5:40; John 2:15-16).

Jesus, when He arrived at Jairus' home, drove out the crowd making fun of Him first, then took the girl's parents and His three disciples into the room holding the girl. In that room and in their presence, Jesus awakened the girl (Mark 5:42–43). This is how God resurrected the church in the sanctuary.

They were both healed at the same time, but the healing of Jairus' daughter is from within. She lost what she used to be and has gained new life. She died from her troubles and had achieved a new identity. They both (the woman & the daughter of Jairus) had the wrong image on them. She was not dead but was sleeping as pointed out by Jesus. She was resting in herself instead of being up and in everyone's face. She was living for the moment that God will call her out of her misery. She changed for the good. God had to change the image on them. Jesus exchanged the life of the woman with that of the daughter of Jairus. Therefore Jesus' remarks in v. 48, *my daughter, your faith has healed you.*

Jesus brought out the daughter (seed) out of the woman as promised in Genesis 3:15. Jesus became the medium for birthing that seed of the woman. Jesus brought that promise to pass. He was the One in-between the creation and the Creator. He brought all those promises in Genesis 3:15 to pass in our time.

The daughter of Jairus was the church that was dying, and Jairus' faith brought the church back on her feet. Jairus was the man who planted the church in the field and was in charge of the church, but his dream was dying in front of his own eyes. So, Jairus reached out to the Lord for help, and that help came in the form of man, Jesus. Jesus brought that church together and lived together as one. The Lord brought the church together—healing and awakening.

God will birth the church-to-come (the seed of the woman) from the now-church. It is this daughter of Jairus who is going to bruise the head of the serpent as pronounced in Genesis 3: 15.

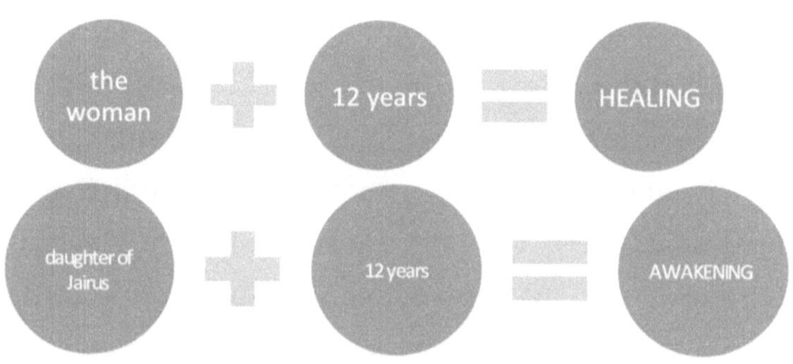

Just as the daughter of Jairus (seed of the woman) was being born at that time the curse was being pronounced on the serpent, the woman with the issue of blood entered into her condition. As the woman grew over the twelve years, she went through different phases of faith. She went through different beliefs—from one doctor to another. She spent all her money through her journey, and then she discovered who Jesus Christ is. The church discovered how to be a Christian—a believer in Jesus Christ.

The woman started from the crushing crowd to discovering the wounds on Jesus' back. The church maneuvered from the other sides of Jesus to the back of Him to touch the border of His garment. The church worked around Jesus until she found the right entry to His soul. The now-church "shifted!" It discovered the stripes of Jesus and followed Him from behind, as others are following Him from the other sides. The woman followed the principles of God set in the Bible to get her healing.

Just as the now-church gets healed, the church-to-come which grew weary and tired fell asleep. And as the woman got healed, the now-church awakened from her sleep. She gained strength from the power transferred from touching the border of Jesus' garment. The church resurrected from her sleep. She grew to be the accepted church of God; *My Daughter*!

God awakened the church through the woman. He called the church-to-come forward. The church is subject to faith. The now-church shifted in her belief. You have the woman in the daughter—the church-to-come growing out of the now-church. The church-to-come will be based on the faith of Jesus Christ. They will build their hope and faith in Jesus. The church will awaken from her flaws.

The Awakening!

In order to awaken the daughter of Jairus, the woman with the issue of blood has to be healed first. The now-church has to be healed first before any resurrection of the Lord's church. The church needs healing from her faults. She has deviated a lot from her faith; that is, the principles of the Bible. She is straying quite widely away from her principles. That is why the Lord needs the church to be healed in the right direction.

She is changing, and this is quite scary as the church is moving into the circle of liars and demonstrators. They are changing the face of the church into something else, but the Lord is great in all things. He will bring us back to Him, in the new age. He will change the face of the church soon in Jesus' name.

> *Jesus went into the Temple and drove out all those who were buying and selling there. He overturned the tables of the moneychangers and the stools of those who sold pigeons, and said to them, "It is written in the Scriptures that God said, 'My Temple will be called a house of prayer.' But you are making it a hideout for thieves!"*
> (John 2:14-17)

This is the reason for the appearance of the woman in the middle of the text before the awakening of the daughter. In the text, the daughter emerged first before the woman. The daughter is ill and dying, but to save the daughter, the woman within has to be healed from her illness; therefore, the coming in-between the daughter's healing.

The Awakening of the Church Age!

In order to awaken the church, all need to have the same faith. The daughter's condition was made known, but before Jesus went to heal her, the woman within her had to be healed of her condition first. So, you see:

1. The daughter of Jairus been mentioned, then
2. The woman with the issue, and then
3. The daughter's awakening.

The woman had to be mentioned in order to save the daughter. In other words, the woman coming in-between the daughter's healing—the awakening of the church in the church—the bringing of divine manifestation to the church of the hill (Calvary). The Lord has brought us to this place of manifestation, and within this manifestation, He will resurrect His church through us. So, although we are with Christ, we are not Christ, and the day that the Christ within us will rise, our destiny will also change as well.

The coming of the church is strange but the divine nature of hers is complex. We are the church in God's eyes but our destiny is within the church, and unless we bring the church forth, our destiny will be held in us. We are to preach the word of God to man and change the destiny of man; if not, our destiny will remain unchanged due to the suppressive nature of man. We are to bring the church forth, and the only way to do it is to preach the word of God to man. We are His laborers in the field, cultivating His land, and as such, have to work wholeheartedly. It is our mandate as a child of God. Principles must be adhered to, and we are God's children, so that must be obeyed. We are obeying God in His field, and we are obeying to keep His will as our interest. Let the will of the Lord be your interest and teach His word.

Liberty comes at a cost—a cost to your freedom. You need to give up your freedom for your liberty. What does that mean, giving up your freedom for your liberty? You need to forfeit your freedom for the cost of your liberty. God created us for Himself and brought us out when we disobeyed Him, but He did not put an end to us. He created a way out for us, and it is that way we called our freedom. Without that way, we will never achieve our liberty from the enemy.

To come out from this, we have to give up the freedom we have now in exchange for the liberty we will gain. The time is coming. So, it is not immediate gratification. You will benefit from your sacrifice when the time comes, but as we are now, we have to give our all to Him, who sees our sacrifice and pays (restores) us back in abundance. For now, let's work for the Lord in establishing His kingdom, and at the right time, He will restore our abundance.

Matthew 6:31-34 (NIV) says;

"So do not worry, saying, 'What shall we eat?' or 'What shall we drink?' or 'What shall we wear?' For the pagans run after all these things, and your heavenly Father knows that you need them. But seek first his kingdom and his righteousness, and all these things will

be given to you as well. Therefore do not worry about tomorrow, for tomorrow will worry about itself. Each day has enough trouble of its own."

What is the cost of our freedom? It all lies within the benefits we reap after the sacrifice. We are sacrificing ourselves for the will of God, so shall the reaping be. We will reap our benefit to sustain us till the end. Sacrificing is a big issue, but paying back for what you sacrificed is amazing. You count your blessings and wildly amazed as to what the Lord has done in place of your sacrifice. It always pays to sacrifice for a good cause.

The Faith of the church

The church must come to believe in whom God has sent, Jesus Christ. They must believe in God, the Father. The faith of the church must be in God. The sheep, pigeons, and the cattle (John 2:14-17) are in the sanctuary for a reason. They represent the needy, the lost, the poor, the sick, and their sacrifices. They are all in the house of God, but the shepherds of the church are leading them astray by selling them to the world.

A temple could be any place the word of God is preached or shared. It can be any corner of a tent or hidden place, as long as the word of God is preached, the presence of God is there. Changing the constitutions of the church does not change the principles of God; it always remains the same regardless of where it is.

A church is a church, and the Temple of God is the Temple of God. You cannot interchange them; the Temple of God is not to be tampered with. You can bring anything into the church. As far as the church is concerned, people come in and out anyhow, but the Temple of God has to be kept sacred for God's purpose only.

Do not confuse the Temple of God with the church; a church comes with her flaws, but the Temple of God is for God and drives all evil out. Just like the outer court of the tabernacle, so is the church on earth. It is full of trespasses and needs cleansing.

Jesus said in Matthew 12:13 that He hasn't come to abolish the Law but to make it clearer for our understanding. There are three parts to the tabernacle; the part that Jesus sits and the part that the mercy seat sits. You cannot bring the outer court into where Jesus sits, and you cannot enter where the mercy seat sits without going through Jesus Christ. You need Christ in all stages of your life. He lives in the holy place of the tabernacle to bring clarification to you about the Law, and He resides in the Holy of Holies with His Father to bring meaning to your life.

In order to go through sanctification, you must come through Christ and to see Jesus; you must understand the law and its principles. Christ did not die on the cross to bring fame to you but to bring you to eternal rest with the Father. That is the story of the cross and resurrection. You cannot preach the word of God without knowing who Jesus is.

Liberating man from the hands of the enemy is what Jesus did by going to the cross on Calvary. He did not go there all by His will, but He ventured on that journey to bring liberation or peace to you to fight the war with the enemy; you have to be on the side of Jesus to fight. You cannot be on the side of the world to fight the enemy.

The world belongs to him, and the church belongs to God, so you cannot claim salvation in the world. You have to come out of the world to gain your salvation. You cannot be a child of God in the world of vultures when the word of God says you cannot sit in the seat of mockers (Psalms 1:1).

You will have to come out, and that is the process that is difficult; coming out of the world into the house of God. That is a difficult adventure; it involves a lot: sacrifices, giving up everything you are or have for the world of God—a very great adventure. But the Lord is saying He will pay you back in abundance all that you lost in His name. You will claim back everything you lost in His name.

It is a painful journey considering leaving everything you have gained in the world for the word of God; everything. He will pay you back in your pregnancy. That is the reason why you are pregnant with His word and you are carrying His word everywhere you go. You are yet to deliver the word, but the word is heavy and difficult to carry around, and it is causing you pain and sorrow, but you are to carry this to the finish. God has implanted this word in you to give to His church, but the word is so difficult to carry around every day—going to church, work, and doing your everyday chore. The word is weighing you down, and then one faithful day the word is birthed to you in excitement, what will you do?

The Lord is waiting for you to birth the word He has given you. Pregnancy is not an easy journey, but you will eventually come to your labor day and on that day, your birth will be glorious to the glory of God. He shall replenish all that you lost during your pregnancy. He births the church in good time.

Follow your heart and be a good steward of the faith. It shall come to an end! Faithful servants are hard to find, but the Lord knows His own. Be of good cheer!

Leaders of the church are not replenishing the faith of the people. They are giving them false hope, but hope is in God, who gives all to mankind. Have faith in Jesus Christ, and all your hopes will come through. Church is for man and not the other way around.

We are to worship God and not the other way around. We are God's people and must obey His words in full. It is only God who will show you which way to go and not man. Have faith in Him who created you. Have faith in Jesus Christ and yourself to be a good shepherd. The will of the Lord is within us, bring it to light!

CHAPTER FIVE

The Woman and the World She Left Behind

> *Then the woman, seeing that she could not go unnoticed, came trembling and fell at his feet. In the presence of all the people, she told why she had touched him and how she had been instantly healed.*
>
> **(Luke 8:47; NIV)**

The world that the woman left behind is about the thoughts of the woman and the love that she had in her heart. This woman has been moving from place to place seeking for healing but to no avail until she met love, Jesus Christ. The woman chose the Son of God over the world. She had a change of heart and pursued the Son of God. She changed her destiny for that of God. She relieved her destiny. There was a time when I used to go to church because it was the right thing to do, but now, I go to church for what the Lord has taught me—His love. He has kept me close to Him, and now I worship Him regardless of my situation. Not the world's situation, but my situation. That is what you call love for the Word. You cannot change the Word of God for that of the world. They are not the same, but they are preached the same. You cannot tell the difference. They might look the same but are not the same. That is the problem with the church today; they take anyone's word for it and do not test it.

The world is full of fear. Check who you dine with and who you present yourself to. The preachers of this World are canning and dangerous. They are everywhere, and you cannot tell the difference between the preachers of the Word of God and that of the World. They are different in the world but are similar in the church. Can you tell who they are? They are in the world ministering to people and lying to people but can you tell who they are? They are all the same in the church.

The Word She Chose

With the crowd almost crushing in on Jesus, it was only the woman with the issue of blood who came up from behind to touch Jesus' garment even as the crowd got bigger. It was only her; the rest just kept on doing their thing. But who is going to save Him from the crowd? As Jesus answered Pilate in the Book of John chapter 19 verse 11 that he only has power over Him because Pilate was given the power by His Father. Either than that, Pilate does not have power over Him. So, who is bigger than Jesus to rescue Him from the hands of the enemy aside God?

God's hand was all along in the crucifixion of His Son on the cross. He initiated and finished it—author and finisher of our faith. God knew what was going to happen and planned it carefully so that the Lord would be crucified at that place; Place of the Skull. God brought Jesus to that place in His life to be crucified by the soldiers, and on that day, He was crucified. He had everything in place so that the world will know that He is God and that He has power over the world. He is great in all His ways and brings unity in a broken place.

So, why can't we live according to the will of God? It seems like an impossible task, but it is feasible. The problem is in our nature, the reason Christ died to that nature is so that you and I can go to the cross and live according to the will of God. You can live according to the will of God if you listen to His word at all time and not make a move without His word. You can live according to the will of God if you give Him your will.

You cannot save the world as people say they are, without the Word of God—critical thinking. You cannot share the world with the devil without knowing who he is. You need to know the word of God.

So, all the leaders who are crying for the world need to know the Word of God before making promises because the world as it is, is more complicated than you think, and very shallow-minded people govern the world. And that is sickening because they do not know the Word of God which created the world and all the things that are in it (John 1:1-3). Understanding is the word! You cannot change the world without the Word of God, and people are claiming to be doing so.

Man harbors wickedness in his heart, and with this wickedness, he reaches out to the church. Man is wicked in his heart. What is this world? It is the world where everyone is in need of God, but they have belittled Him. They have brought Him to a place where He cannot be reached. That is the church today. They have crucified Jesus and have made Him invisible to the crowd. Although the crowd is almost caving in on Jesus, they cannot tell who He is because of their false idea of who He is.

The church is in great crisis today. She is living in the world instead of the world living by her Word. That is the church today! She is leaving behind her principles. The church is in her dying stage, but God is great to bring life to her. The church today is in great crisis. She is dying of her sin and capturing the sin of the world. She is living according to the sin of the world. She has given up her principles and imbibed the principles of the world.

She is mounting a hill that is so steep to climb that she cannot hold on to it. She is slipping back. The church is in Christ, but Christ is not in the church. It is the reason the church is slipping from the Word of God—the church that the woman left behind. The woman with the issue of blood lived in that church with others; the crowd. The crowd came waiting to see Jesus as witnesses. They have heard about Him but do not know where to place Him. The crowd who came waiting to see Jesus did not know who He was until He died on the cross. In Luke

23, before Jesus died on the cross, the whole crowd including the chief priests, the leaders, and the people demanded Jesus to be crucified after Pilate appealed to the crowd to set Him free. After Jesus died on the cross, the crowd beat their chest in regret. The world does not know who God is, but the church does. That is the weirdest thing. The church knowing who God is and denying Him, and the world rejecting Him for who He is—that is the story. That is what the cross talks about—the rejection of Christ. The world rejected Him, and the church denied Him.

The church of today is like that. No one respects God in His sanctuary. Man comes to the sanctuary to worship God, but they do not worship God. They worship their own image in the sanctuary. The sanctuary of God has turned into the devil worshippers' place. They incarnate the word of God and create their own misery in place of God's word. They are just church-goers and not believers in Christ. The Bible says in John Chapter 2 verse 13 through 22 that when Jesus cleansed the Temple in Jerusalem of its moneychangers, He did so by making <u>a whip from cords,</u> and with that whip, He drove out all the animals and overturned the table of the moneychangers from the Temple. Jesus changed the destiny of the Temple.

It was almost time for the Passover Festival, so Jesus went to Jerusalem. There in the Temple, he found people selling cattle, sheep, and pigeons, and also the moneychangers sitting at their tables. So he made a whip from cords and drove all the animals out of the Temple, both the sheep and the cattle; he overturned the tables of the moneychangers and scattered their coins; and he ordered those who sold the pigeons, "Take them out of here! Stop making my Father's house a marketplace!" His disciples remembered that the scripture says, "My devotion to your house, O God, burns in me like a fire." The Jewish authorities came back at him with a question, "What miracle can you perform to show us that you have the right to do this?" Jesus answered, "Tear down this Temple, and in three days I will build it again." "Are you going to build it again in three days?" they asked him. "It has taken forty-six years to build this Temple!" But the temple Jesus was speaking about was his body. So when he was raised from death, his disciples remembered that he had said this, and they believed the scripture and what Jesus had said. (John 2:13–22; GNT)

When Jesus was challenged and questioned about His right for cleansing the Temple of its moneychangers and animals, He answered them by challenging them to tear down His body, which is the Temple of God, and He will rebuild it in three days. He was not talking about His ability to come to life and change things, but He was speaking about His ability to bring life into dead things. He changed the life of the church after His resurrection. He rebuilds the church in three days. He resurrected the church in three days. In three days, He brought the church back on her feet. But first, the Jewish authorities had to tear down His body, which they did by the journey He made to the cross. They proved to Him that they could tear down His body, but they were waiting for Him to prove His side of the deal by rebuilding the body in three days. Jesus did so by healing the woman with the issue of blood. As the Bible says in Genesis chapter three; God says He will bring enmity between the serpent and the woman, but the seed of the woman will crush the serpent's head, and the serpent will bruise her seed's heel. That is the story of this journey that Jesus is on; bringing divinity to the word of God. The church is to tear the body of Christ down, and the body of Christ is to heal the church in three days.

As the Jewish authorities said, it has taken them forty-six years to build the Temple that Jesus cleansed of moneychangers. It has taken the world that long to build the church you see now with its moneychangers and corruptions. It all started from somewhere and built up to where it is now. It has taken the world that long to gradually creep into the church of God to change her principles to that of the world, and now, Jesus is saying He can rebuild the church in three days if it is torn down. How is He going to do this? Forty-six years versus three days!

So, they went on the challenge. Jesus' body was beaten, wounded, torn down, and bled by the crowd. The Temple died (telling you the state of the church to come), was buried, and on the third day, rose again. The temple was torn down by the very crowd that almost crushed in on Him. The fact that someone follows Christ does not mean they are for Christ. There are a lot of followers of Christ, but fewer believers.

The Crowd

Pilate spoke again to the crowd, "What, then, do you want me to do with the one you call the king of the Jews?" They shouted back, "Crucify him!" "But what crime has he committed?" Pilate asked. They shouted all the louder, "Crucify him!" Pilate wanted to please the crowd, so he set Barabbas free for them. Then he had Jesus whipped and handed him over to be crucified.
(Mark 14: 12–5; GNT)

The chief priests and the whole Council tried to find some evidence against Jesus in order to put him to death, but they could not find any. Many witnesses told lies against Jesus, but their stories did not agree. Then some men stood up and told this lie against Jesus: "We heard him say, 'I will tear down this Temple which men have

*made, and after three days I will build one that
is not made by men.'" Not even they, however,
could make their stories agree.*
(Mark 14: 55–59)

The crowd in Luke 8:42 were almost caving in on Jesus but not touching His garment. They surrounded Him but were not serving Him accordingly. They lived for themselves alone and not for Christ. They are the churches of today. They only live for themselves. They have surrounded Him, Jesus Christ, basing their religion and ideology on Him, but are not worshipping Him. What do you think about this? There are people in the church who cry for the Lord but are not with the Lord. Why, because they do not know Him as Jesus Christ. They have heard His name just as the crowd has done but do not know who He really is. They came to follow Him, to see for themselves who people say He is but have not taken the time to actually know Him. They are basing their knowledge of who He is on who they think He is but not who He really is. Lots of churches are being built today; countless of them but based on what foundation? What are their beliefs and purpose for setting up these churches in the name of Jesus? What are the building blocks of these churches crushing in on Jesus Christ? Are they for Jesus Christ?

The crowd from all walks of life beset Jesus. They have all come to see Jesus, but how many of them are really like Jesus? Because Jesus says if you know my Father, you know Me. So,

Jesus is the incarnation of God on earth. What authority has He got to say that? That authority is in His nature. That is why He is God and man in nature. He carries the authority of God in Him and the authority of man on Him. If you tear down the body, you tear down the authority of man on Him, and then the authority of God prevails. Killing His body does not kill God, but rather, it kills the nature of man on Him. Crushing in on Jesus Christ brought out the nature of God in Him. He rebuilds the body in three days by God's authority on Him as the Christ after the body has been torn down.

This is how Jesus is going to rebuild the church after we tear it down. We are tearing it down by our own strength. There are churches upon churches, all of them claiming the word of God, but which of the word of God, the truth? The churches surround Jesus Christ but are not touching the hem of His garment. None of the churches is coming from behind to touch the hem of Jesus' garment. No one wants to experience the suffering that Jesus went through for the sake of the gospel. Everyone wants to bypass the sufferings and go straight to the restoration, but it does not work that way. Now, you see churches escaping the cross for the restoration. They live the life of the world. They think about nothing but the wealth of the world. They have created their own god, and this god brings them wealth instead of peace, but the peace of the Lord is what you need. Man cannot live in this world without peace. Peace brings us together, and without peace, man lives in this world with no hope. Everything man does is to please the world that he lives in. There is no gratification in life. The life of man is based on the principles the world has given him.

The churches almost crushing in on Jesus are not touching the stripes on His back to regain power over the world. They are walking with Jesus, but are not with Him. As God showed me in a dream couple of years ago, there were two tubs of identical body creams. In my eyes, both tubs contained the same product, and their outer packaging is the same. The Lord then asked me to apply the cream from each tub on a separate leg, which I did. Then He asked me, *can you tell the difference between the two creams on your legs?* I took a look at both legs, and they all looked the same. I could not tell them apart because they all gave the same effect after the application. *I could not tell them apart*, I answered, but the Lord said, *they are not all the same.* One is an imitation of the other; it appears the same, but they are not alike. That was what God was trying to say to me, that a time is coming and it is here, that man will not be able to tell the truth from the false. The church says she has surrounded Jesus Christ but which of the Jesus? Is it Jesus Christ of Nazareth? The church may seem to be occupied with God's work but which God are they working for; the god of this world or the God of Life? This is the problem with the church today; we have surrounded things that are not meant for us but the world and we are competing with the world for their place. We are crushing in on Jesus, but we are not coming behind to touch the hem of His garment.

The Christ we need to follow is the One with the stripes of suffering on His back. He has our salvation all written on His back with the wounds He suffered for our sake.

> *Dear friends, do not believe every spirit, but test the spirits to see whether they are from God, because many false prophets have gone out into the world. This is how you can recognize the Spirit of God: Every spirit that acknowledges that Jesus Christ has come in the flesh is from God, but every spirit that does not acknowledge Jesus is not from God. This is the spirit of the antichrist, which you have heard is coming and even now is already in the world.*
> (1 John 4:1–3; NIV)

The church is breaking down the Body of Christ, but how? All the principles in the church are changing. The church is taking on the principles of the world. This is how the church is deceiving God (but God cannot be deceived nor mocked) by giving up her principles for that of the world. But God says that the seed of the woman will crush the head of the serpent, so God has developed a way whereby man will gain his independence back from the enemy, and that seed and independence is Jesus Christ. Believing in Jesus Christ and understanding His word will bring independence to you; until then, man will be in the clutches of the serpent. The church needs this independence because a time is coming when man will find no peace in the land. Man will search everywhere in the land; the places he used to go to find peace will be overgrown with thorn bushes (Isaiah 7:23–25).

This is how the church is going to turn out to be, a hell place, but salvation is at Golgotha or "the Place of the Skull." If you can reach that place, you will find peace in you. The last days of the church are incredible. Things are going to change in the church, but the ones that will be left standing will be the ones that can withstand the test of times. Difficult years are approaching the church. Things are going to change in the church, but the truth is, how are you going to withstand the changes? The church is being handed to the world, how are we going to protect the church from falling? The principles of the church are going to fall, how are you going to help her from falling apart?

Do not let what you see in the church now fool you because consequences are going to follow our actions. Difficult times are coming! It is a calamity that is going to befall the church, but the church will come out of it. It is something that has to happen to birth the new church out of the old. The church is in deep trouble but how are we going to bring ourselves out of this disaster? We need God!

Do not break the bond you have with Jesus Christ, always do the work of God.

The woman with the issue of blood
chose the Word over the World.

Thinking about the journeys people make on countless occasions to Israel to see the Holy Land, what is their reason for traveling, because you do not see the place as you should? Then it dawns on me that people do not have the heart to love God, but they have the heart to visit places they think the Son of God has visited. That is the trouble of the world today; they chase after wealth but not the Creator of the wealth. It is all right to visit the place but be sure you have the Lord in your heart. There is no point in visiting the place when your love for the Lord has gone out of your heart. You cannot replace your knowledge of who Christ is by visiting His footprints. You need to be pure in heart to seek His face. We are making all these journeys but are we right with the Lord? You cannot compensate for your behavior with closure. What are we doing that is diverting our attention from the will of God that we need His reassurance to make us free? You do not visit these places just to seek closure. You cannot seek closure from what you do not know. You need to understand God to find closure in Him. We cannot go to Him and leave our outer covering behind in the world. We go to God without our outer self and seek for closure on pretense. You cannot do that. You must be sincere with yourself and seek what you want from God.

The World and the Cross

The world is in the hands of the enemy, and the cross is in the hands of God. You cannot leave the cross in the hands of the enemy; disaster will happen! That is what is happening to the church now. We have left the cross in the hands of the enemy. Therefore, disaster is coming upon us, the church. How can you leave what belongs to God in the hands of the enemy? He will trash it. The church is in ruins, but the Lord will save her.

The church is meant to carry the cross of Christ on her back, but she is carrying the demise of the world. The world does not care for the cross of Calvary, neither the church these days. The church is replacing her principles with that of the world. They do not care about the cross on Calvary; all they care about is the will of the world. The church is building her gates against the word of God. She is driving the Word of God out of herself and replacing it with worldly things. There is no more sympathy in the church and diversity is a thing of the past in the church nowadays. They are all following the world's true colors.

Beware of the betrayers of the Word of God! The Lord will bring the barber of the Emperor of Assyria on the church. He will shave every hair on the body of the church. You need the cross to bring salvation to man. So, where is the church with salvation? We need the cross to bring salvation to the church, but the cross is in the hand of the enemy. How are we going to bring or turn around when the church's destiny is in the hands of the enemy? We cannot let go of things when the church's destiny is in the hands of the enemy. How do you bring yourselves out of this curse? It is all by the grace of God which He has showered us with. The will of God is to bring all churches together, but how is it going to be done when all church is doing is bring division? The church is closing her gate to the word of God.

The world is changing! The cries of the nations are reaching God, and He is answering their cries, but are the nations happy with His answers? God is creating a system whereby His nations will be exonerated from their troubles and bring them to the level that He is, but are the nations happy? The nations are the churches in God (Genesis 17: 4-6). A church is not just a place of communion, but it is a place where the people go to bring peace to themselves. The world is wreaking so much havoc in the church. Religions are changing to bring in the values of the world, but what is the point of having a religion if you cannot control what goes in and out of it? The days when religion used to be a master of peace is gone. It is now filled with eccentrics of the world. The population in the church is changing.

Tithes are created for man and not man for the tithes. We are living in an age where people dictate what other people should do. The world is in chaos, so is the church that God has built upon His name. The church principles are changing, and the attitudes of the church have changed. God is no more in these churches. Churches are not what we think they should be. A church is a place where the word of God is shared. It could be anywhere, as long as the word of God is shared, God presence will be there. But the church is now dividing into many sections that you do not understand. The word of God is for all nations, and not for one nation. We are all to listen to His word and find a way of bringing us together. We are all God's children, and the world is crushing us into its pit. Let us bring ourselves together and establish the church that God has spoken about. The church is in God's hands, and the enemy is on the loose looking for people to betray the Son of God, Jesus Christ. God is among us and with us. Let the church be your priority! Help build the church of God; differentiation will not help and will destroy the church of God. Do not discriminate because you do not know who God is in your midst. Share the word of God among yourselves! Teach the word to the poor and change the hearts of people.

Mark 16:14-15; NIV says; "*Later Jesus appeared to the Eleven as they were eating; he rebuked them for their lack of faith and their stubborn refusal to believe those who had seen him after he had risen. He said to them, "Go into all the world and preach the gospel to all creation.*

Acts 17:24-31; NIV says: "*The God who made the world and everything in it is the Lord of heaven and earth and does not live in temples built by human hands. And he is not served by human hands, as if he needed anything. Rather, he himself gives everyone life and breath and everything else. From one man he made all the nations, that they should inhabit the whole earth; and he marked out their appointed times in history and the boundaries of their lands. God did this so that they would seek him and perhaps reach out for him and find him, though he is not far from any one of us.*

'For in him we live and move and have our being.' As some of your own poets have said, 'We are his offspring.' "Therefore since we are God's offspring, we should not think that the divine being is like gold or silver or stone—an image made by human design and skill. In the past God overlooked such ignorance, but now he commands all people everywhere to repent. For he has set a day when he will judge the world with justice by the man he has appointed. He has given proof of this to everyone by raising him from the dead."

The Confirmation

While Jesus was saying to the woman, "My daughter, your faith has made you well. Go in peace," a messenger came from Jairus' house announcing the death of Jairus' daughter. The pronunciation of peace and confirmation of the <u>faith</u> over the woman coincided with the announcement of the death of Jairus' daughter.

V. 50 - *But Jesus heard it and said to Jairus, "Don't be afraid; <u>only believe</u>, and she will be well."*

The toughest words and task are "to believe"! How do you believe when everything is falling apart? How do you believe in something that you do not have faith in? That is our problem with the church and her offspring. The churches "belief system" has been corrupted by the very people who are to build our faith and belief in the Word of God. The bearers of the Word have shattered our faith. The church is falling apart due to unbelief, and the church is not doing anything about it. How do you shape the church? How many of these churches speak the word of God? The church is changing in her belief, and it is about time the church stands up to the world and return to her principles. But that is going to be difficult because the church is in the world and the world is leading the church. Can any change take place? No, because we are in the world and until we come out of the world's principles, the church will always remain in the world. The principles are changing, and we are seeing the church moving further into the world. Is this what God intended for the church, or are we not trespassing God's rules? The church is God's, and we have to meet His principles in the church. The belief system has become an issue since we live in the eyes of the world. Change must happen! The woman is bleeding and needs healing!

How do you cope with your unbelief? Jesus said to the woman; it was her faith that has healed her-only believe! Do not just be a follower, but a believer. It was faith that made the woman touched Jesus. Are we touching Jesus' garment or just following Him? Being a follower of Jesus Christ does not guarantee you are touching His garment. All the people around denied touching the hem of His garment. Not every follower of Christ is a potential believer in Him. The crowd are all following Him, but do they all believe in Him as the Christ? This is the question, "Who touched me?" asked Jesus. *Who touched my garment?* Belief is a question here. Who believed in Me so much to touch my garment? So, all the people waiting for Him on the other side when Jesus arrived did not believe in Him except the woman. She came up from the crowd behind Jesus to touch

His garment. That is a mystery, isn't it? As poor as she is, she gave all her money for healing but got nothing back but failure. She is poor in heart but still looking for the Messiah. Amazing how the trust of people fades in the storms of life. They easily forget, but God is good; He brings resurrection to the poor in heart because of their faith. Their faith will bring them peace in their days.

To be a follower of Jesus Christ, your cause has to be like that of Jesus—touch Him and trust Him. Are we true Christians or not? Are you just following Jesus or participating in His cause? Do we believe in Jesus or not? If we do, we would not just be following Him but touching His garment to draw power out of Him. It is this power that we will win us this land back—get our freedom back. The power of Jesus is in our reach. It is only by faith that you can access this power for healing. Trust in Jesus to receive your healing.

Touch the power of God to receive your healing!

CHAPTER SIX

The Church and the Cross

> *"And he ordered those who sold the pigeons,*
> *"Take them out of here! Stop making my Fa-*
> *ther's house a marketplace!"*
> **(John 2:16; GNT)**

God is for all, and He has this universe in His plan. He created all these for His purpose. God knows about all these things happening in the church and knows about how it will end. It is amazing how every religion in the land talks about a god. They show reverence to this god who is everything to them, but the god they worship is the god they believe in. Religion is just a platform to grasp an idea of God but knowing God is by fellowshipping with Him.

There are churches upon churches all waiting on a messiah; someone to deliver them from their stress. These churches live in distress but not in their religion. How you view the Messiah is all based on your need. He will be who He is to you according to your need. For instance, if you are seeking for love; love will be your Savior, and if you are seeking for hatred; hatred will be your Savior. Depending on what you seek, that need becomes your Savior. You build your faith upon your belief (1 Corinthians 3:11; Matthew 16:13–20). The church's faith is tied to the church they belong to but not who they believe in. That is all about church! So, you have many churches sprouting up from different beliefs, and this is where our problems come from; different beliefs.

The churches are everywhere, surrounding everyone, but the beliefs in the churches are different. That is why God is warning us against disbelief. All these churches have surrounded themselves with a belief, and a belief that God is great but they are forgetting that God created the universe and that all His children are one. So, if you believe in God, you should also have faith in Jesus who He has birthed to us.

You cannot love God and disown your neighbor; we are all one church, no one is better than the other. It is just a misunderstanding; so surrounding Jesus are the churches, all using Him as a pivot to support their faith. But what is their faith, that is what Jesus is asking, "Who touched me"? They believe that one day a Messiah will show up and rescue them from the hands of the enemy, that is the whole story—a being will rescue them.

On the other side of the lake, the crowd welcomed Jesus because they were there waiting for Him (the Messiah). They were so on to Jesus because they have a need and have heard about Him. He is a form of a messiah. All these churches are crowding in on Jesus, but none has faith in Jesus as to touch Him as the Messiah until the woman with the issue of blood touched the hem of His garment. This was when they declared their alliance with Jesus. Until then, they were almost caving in on Him. When Jesus asked "who touched me," everyone denied touching Him, but He knew someone had touched Him, and there the woman confessed of touching His garment.

We are all looking for a Savior some way, somehow, and in some form according to our need, but this Savior is close to us; walking with us just that we do not know it is Him. What do we need to see before we believe? The churches are all around Jesus, but their beliefs are stopping them from touching the hem of His garment. How is God going to bring these beliefs together as one? Jesus healed the woman with the issue of blood. He healed her disbelief with belief. How did He do it?

God healed her by turning all her sorrows into joy. He placed love in her, and that love conquered everything in her to bring peace to her. That is what God is going to do with the churches in the land; they are many and with different beliefs but God will bring them together as one, and God's universe will be formed (Genesis 1:1). He brings the churches into one fold and under one Shepherd; the awakening of the daughter of Jairus.

So, what Jesus did with the temple in Jerusalem (John 2:13–16); He will do it again in order to save the church in the end. "Salvation belongs to God!"

The Woman with No Name

Who is this woman with no name? The text says she came up in the crowd behind Jesus. This is the woman with multiple issues in her life. She realized who Jesus is and touched His garment for healing—the healing that brought all the churches together in Jesus' name! The healing that is meant for the church-to-come. Discrimination and destruction are not allowing us to sit back and analyze our actions and thoughts.

How do we think about Jesus and who He is? How do we analyze His strength? The Bible has said many things about Jesus, the Messiah, but we have not taken the time to find out who He is. He is everyone's Savior according to your need. He cannot be the church. Otherwise, we will not worship, but He is the One in whom the fullness of the Godhead dwells bodily, a Deliverer of this world. Churches are fighting over churches because their faith is better than the other, but what is your faith? Is your faith any better than the other? Is your belief deeper than them? We are all God's creation and therefore, worship the God that we serve but with different views of what God is to us. Division is not good for the church, as Jesus said in John 2:16, "Stop making my Father's house a marketplace!" (GNT).

The woman with no name came up in the crowd behind to touch Jesus' garment to bring out what the church desires out from Jesus—power and love. The woman in the text has no name because she belongs to no one but God. The Bible did not name her because she is for all. She is not set for a particular race, religion, tribe, social class or intellect. She is the church;

the house of God, a belief that no one understands except God Himself. The woman is to bring hope to us and assure us of the will of God (Luke 8:47). We all believe in One person—the Most High God!

This is the woman in the text of Genesis 3, the "desire" of God. What is the desire of God? The desire of God is the church—that is why He said to the woman in Genesis 3 that "your desire will still be for your husband." The desire of God is the church. In John 2:17, the text says "His disciples remembered that the scripture says, 'My devotion to your house, O God, burns in me like a fire.'"

The woman is going through an issue of blood because of all the things that are happening in her life. She is losing blood because of all that is happening to the church. These changes are draining her of blood. Blood is essential for life. She is energetically drained, but she is still carrying on as a woman that she is. She keeps on going because she knows there is a cure out there. She persevered with her issue. She is bleeding; the church is bleeding of the very thing that is to keep her alive. She is losing everything she has or owns. She is going through a period where everything she has worked for is being lost through this issue of blood. But she brought peace of Jesus Christ to herself. She exchanged her problems for the peace of God. That is the reason for the coming of Jesus Christ; to bring the church the peace of God. The destiny of the church was changed to love.

> *Then the Lord God made the man fall into a*
> *deep sleep, and while he was sleeping, he took*
> *out one of the man's ribs and closed up the flesh.*
> *He formed a woman out of the rib and brought*
> *her to him. Then the man said, "At last, here*
> *is one of my own kind— Bone taken from my*
> *bone, and flesh from my flesh. 'Woman' is her*
> *name because she was taken out of man.*
> **(Genesis 2:21-23; GNT)**

The woman is Eve, as Adam named her after the fall in the Garden of Eden because she was the mother of all living. She is the church today crying out to God for help. She changed her destiny, but how?

> *Adam named his wife Eve, because she was*
> *the mother of all living.*
> **(Genesis 3:20)**

What happened to the church?

The woman mentioned at the beginning of the Bible is seen eating some of the fruit of the evil tree. First, she <u>sees</u> with her eyes how beautiful the tree is, acknowledges how good its fruit will be to eat, and <u>thought</u> how desirable it is to be wise. Then you see her taking some of the fruit of this tree and eating it. Before this happened, she confessed the law of the garden to the serpent; about how God has said to them to eat fruits from any tree in the garden except the tree in the middle of the garden.

God says we are not to eat its fruits or touch it. But in Genesis 3:6, the text says when she saw how beautiful this evil tree was, and she thought how wonderful it would be to be wise, she ate some of its fruit. Does that mean that she never set her eyes on this tree or she saw this beauty in this tree from a different angle as described by the serpent?

She saw something in the tree that she had never seen before because the serpent spoke to her. She used her eyes to see the other side of the tree that is prohibited to them and used her mind to conclude how wonderful it would be to be wise. She made all these judgments based on the statement that the serpent made to her (Genesis 3:4).

She changed the course of her life by simply making judgment based on what she heard with her ears. She did not check it with the information given by God. She took some of its fruit, ate it, and offered some to her husband, and he also ate it. From that very moment, their eyes opened by gaining understanding and realization of their surroundings. They felt their nakedness, and they covered it with sown fig leaves.

The woman might have seen the tree with a different set of eyes which gave her the conclusion that she came to - A set of eyes that the LORD did not give her; *deception*. This brought their downfall. What the woman with the issue of blood is doing, going through the land is to find a place of belonging, and that is what she found in Jesus Christ. In the beginning was the

Word, the Word was with God, and the Word was God (John 1: 1), that is what the Bible tells us. These are the three stages of our lives as the church.

So, if in the beginning was the Word, and the Word was with God, and the Word was God, then who was God in the beginning? Because in the beginning, there was no sin until sin entered the world through deception, so who was God in the beginning because He surely spoke of the truth.

Then the text says "the Word was with God;" so what happened to the Word? If in the beginning the Word existed and now it says "the Word was with God," meaning the Word was tampered with, and He left the abode of God. What really happened to the truth of God's Word?

Then the Bible goes on to say, "and the Word was God," meaning the truth lies in God. The truth of the Word is God. Is it the truth of Genesis 3:2-3 or Genesis 3:4? The church has been lied to believe in Genesis 3:4 and not Genesis 3:2-3. So, in the beginning:

...Was the Word – It was the innocent age of the church when God established her and gave the church her innocence. God established the church based on the truth of His Word and that His Word shall never depart from us. It will always remain the same—the unchangeable God. Through thick and thin, He will always be here. His Word, that is the Bible, will always remain the same. Not a single word of it will be removed or added (Deuteronomy 4:2; Revelation 22:18), but man changed. God did not change; He has always been the same. He is still God, but we changed.

The Word was with God – the innocence of the church was taken away from her by the deception of the serpent. It changed the course of the church and brought the church to a standstill, with no progress whatsoever in her life. The church was bleeding of her life. This is what happened to the church in her innocence. Her innocence was taken from her, and she started to bleed everywhere she went. The church became a problem in the world because she has listened to the word of the serpent. But she did not only listen to the word but actually participated in its actions; therefore, the LORD's punishment came on her as the LORD says in Revelation 22:18-19. She changed her clothes to that of the serpent and birth deception. But the LORD says in Genesis 3 that the seed of the woman will crush the head of the serpent and what the woman birthed with the serpent will always be enemies with the seed of the woman.

The future and the past of the woman will always be enemies; they will never understand each other. The past of the woman was her innocence, and the future of the woman is the deception that has left her with no innocence. She has been robbed of her youth, and now she is growing old with no dignity. She needs her dignity back shortly.

So, the church turned when she bought the thought of the world. Her idea of church changed from the innocent one to the church with many ideas—in other sense, understanding. So, the church is evolving every single day into something else with different ideologies, worships, understanding, signs, and wonders—the dignity of the church is gone all because of wisdom and understanding.

How can you gain wisdom from the world, when the world does not understand itself? It is preposterous! The church took a different turn and managed her way through the lands and cultivated lies. Deception is crippling the church that she cannot walk on her feet.

The woman is crawling around, trying to be saved, but the word she is carrying is not right. You cannot go through the land with those clothes on you. The church should be wearing the right clothes. Therefore, Jesus changed the clothing on the church and brought peace to her and awoken the innocence in her (Luke 8:54–55).

The church is stepping out of line based on heresy. It is the church that is moving away from God because of her ideologies. She is moving away from God, where she used to be. She has changed her story and preaching according to the world and what pleases the world. She is not going by the Word of God; the fundamental principles of the church.

When a gunman comes to your home and wants to shoot you, will you just say shoot me, or you will struggle with the gunman to get him to change his mind? That is the church today; she takes anything that anyone throws at her. She just takes anything from the world without comparing it with the Word of God.

She has strayed far from God that she needs to come back to God. She needs her life back. She was comfortable in God's hand till she decided to go against the Word of God. She brought herself down and needed deliverance from her sin. The woman is approaching the Word of God closely but cannot reach it. She is leading the world into sin. The woman is touching the world but not the Word of God. She is not saving people's lives.

The principles of the church are changing, but the Bible says in Matthew 24:35 that, "Heaven and earth will pass away, but my words will never pass away" (Deuteronomy 4:2; Revelation 22:18–19). The LORD has spoken about His church and what is to happen in His church, but the modern church is caught between a rock and a hard place. She cannot turn around, although she wishes she could because the deception is too much for the church.

As the Word of God says, heaven and earth will surely pass away, but God's undistinguishable word will never pass away. It will forever remain the same. Through countless generations, this Word of God will always remain unchanged. It will survive through all the different generations of the church, people, ideologies, and technicalities. Not a single word of it will be changed to suit a particular generation. It will survive through all generations of this world and will still come out to be the truth. The Word will not be bent to suit or cover the sins of any generation. It is what it is. Generations will come and go, but the authenticity of the Word of God will remain the same. God has crafted it to suit all generations.

All generations of this world fit into the Bible; it covers everything that is to come into this world. So, you see, you do not have to bend the rules to suit a particular generation but use the Word of God as a ruler to rule the world of its mishaps. Do not change it around. Do not bring the word of the world into the church, but rather take the church into the world and rule it by her principles.

There is no way that church is incapable of ruling the world, the only challenge is, is the world capable of ruling the church? The Bible has been crafted by God for the years to come. God knows who mankind is and He has crafted the Bible to suit our age, so why are we trying to change the Bible that He has crafted in His name to suit our generation? God has the world in His hands. The Bible caters for all generations of this world. God incorporated all generations into the Bible; He had us in mind when He crafted the Bible and knew the generations to come.

And the Word Was God – From generation to generation, the Word is God. God will always prevail. The church started with God and will end with God. The church will always be on the right side of God. The truth will always win the war of our minds. Jesus is the Law laid out for the church to follow. He is the ruler by which the church measures her life. He is the Redeemer because He brought the woman out from the house of evil. He lifted up our souls. He gave us hope and delivered us from the hands of our minds.

He is God in us, and He is the third person in us. He is the resurrected Word of God; the Word that was given to the enemy to turn it whichever way he wanted. He is our Savior and the Messiah of this world because it is based on His word that this world will change. Jehovah is Christ in us, and Jehovah is who we are in Jesus Christ. The Word of God has been given, and the enemy is at large. Change your mind according to the Word of God because the Word is God.

> *"Your word is a lamp to guide me and*
> *a light for my path."*
> **(Psalms 119:105)**

December 20th

This message came to me while I was writing a Christmas piece for my blog about our purpose for celebrating the birth of Jesus. What is the significance of this celebration? This led me to write the inserted message.

"The Message of Christmas!

It is Christmas again, and all Christian churches are celebrating the birth of the Word of God, Jesus Christ. But what are we really celebrating, His birth or His destruction? I do not know where the Christian Church stands now with regards to the word of God that we celebrate every Christmas. We are surely adding our thoughts to His Word. The Bible says in Revelation 22:19 and Deuteronomy 4:2 not to add anything to or remove from His Word. We should reflect on God's word and see where we are as a church with regards to the truth of His Word.

I am saying this because the church seems to obey the word of the world more than it does the Word of God. This is what the Book of Genesis says about how beautiful the tree was when the woman saw it and how good its fruit would be if eaten and thought how wonderful it would be to be wise. Just at the sight of the tree, our thoughts changed. We seem to be moving away from the Word of God. Disobedience is the worst sin in His eyes. If it isn't, He wouldn't have sent Adam and Eve out of the Garden of Eden because of their disobedience. Why will you send your child out of your home if what the child did was just minor? We are exhibiting exactly what happened in the garden in our churches. The truth of the word of God is disappearing in our churches. The truth is not being said.

The church has doubted herself from the time of old till now about the truth of God's word. We have doubted the word that God has given with our thoughts, and we have brought into the church our thoughts. Now, we doubt God more than anyone else, why? This is all in the name of pleasing ourselves and justifying our actions against the Word of God. We have brought doubt into the church.

How Did We Get Here?

"...Now the snake was the most cunning animal that the Lord God had made. The snake

*asked the woman, "**Did God really** tell you **not**
to eat fruit from any tree in the garden?"*
(Genesis 3:1 – Emphasis added)

The serpent planted the seed of doubt in Eve's mind.

*"…did God **really** tell you **not to**…"*

The word of the serpent put man in a place of doubting the authenticity of God's Word. It makes you doubt the word you have received [cognitive process, thinking]. It makes us doubt ourselves of the principles that God has given us to live by. It is an ongoing thing that is happening every single day in our lives; comparing the word of God with the situations in our lives. This story of *doubt* was not only confined to the Garden of Eden, but it reflects in our daily lives with what the Word of God says and what we think of the word—the principles of our living. We are in constant doubt with ourselves because of our nature. We are always comparing our thoughts with the Word of God. We are always comparing what God has said with what we have heard with our ears; trying to make an excuse for our thinking.

The church is found adding her thoughts to the word of God. It is difficult living in the modern church system as everything has to have a meaning relating to the world and not the word of God. We are changing the principles of the church, so what are we celebrating today, the birth of the Word of God, Jesus, or the extension of His Word?

We are living by His Word, aren't we?

The purpose of celebrating the Word of God, Jesus Christ, is to show how we reverence His word, but do we?

Are we as Christians, giving meaning to Christmas?

The Word of God has been birthed to us to obey and live by, but are we listening to and obeying His Word. Jesus has been birth to us for a purpose. We have to have faith in His Word.

How Do You Classify What is Good and What is Bad?

That is all up to God because He knows His Word and knows the world. He created the world and all that is in it and has the authority over it. Checking who is wrong and who is right is up to God but weighing your sin is up to the Son of God. It is by His measure that we live since God created the world based on His Word. God created the world but made you in charge of your decision making. We are to make and base our choices on His word, and adding your thoughts to God's word removes that authority He has on it.

You have given your mind that authority to rule over you. And that is where the church is heading, with decisions being made by our intellect and not the wisdom of God. We add to and take away anything that does not suit us to make things right with our soul. But the word of the LORD is not to be tampered with. It shall forever stay the same as our God is unchangeable (Matthew 5:18). So is His Word.

Think about your actions in the church and check where you are with the Word of God. The times are changing, and divination is in the air.

As the church celebrates Jesus Christ, let us reflect on the Word of God given to us in the Garden of Eden. (Genesis 3:2-3)

The Revelation of Jesus

God's revelation of who Jesus is, is a mystery to the church. He revealed who Jesus was and is in the scriptures (Isaiah 9:6) when He said a Child is born to you and a Son is given to you! God revealed His nature in the text. He said Jesus was a Child born to you, and as a Son given to you. This is the nature of Jesus, and this is the word of God. This is where the revelation of Jesus is. God revealed Himself in that Isaiah 9:6.

God revealed Himself through the scriptures. He showed us who He is and who He will be by stating that statement in the Bible. He purely showed as that as a Child, He will be born to us in our nature, and as a Son, He will be given to us as a choice. We choose who we want to worship, God or the evil one. We have a choice here, but before that time comes, we will be walking with the Child born to us. He will be in His childhood nature. As a church, He will be born to us, and everyone will have access to Him, but the choice of choosing Him as your Savior will be up to the church. They have an option to choose Jesus as their Savior, but literally, you are making your own choice whether to walk with Him or not. That is where the churches go wrong with their choices. They choose God, but shelter for another divine nature. They know of God but do not know who He is.

Some believers in God are selective and make their choice according to their predicament. For instance, they choose wealth as their savior in the days of financial adversity, not total dependence on Him. Therefore, their pseudo-relationship with God is based on NEED, not PURITY. They ONLY pitch their tents with God because He can meet their needs, not because of His Holiness. That is where the problem arises because God is God and you cannot worship any other god beside Him (Exodus 20:3–5).

For this reason, God gave His nature to us on earth; a Child to be born to us so that we on earth can relate to His nature for every need. God brought His Son to us on earth to show but to relieve us of our stress; so pray through Jesus, the Son of God because He is the only relation of God on earth. He is the link between God and man. He has our nature in Him and God's as well. He is us in the word of God.

God revealed Him to us, and we are still asking who He is because He has already placed Him in us as a church. And we are still seeking Him among the crowd. Jesus is with us in our hearts. Searching for the word of God is strange, but He has already been planted in our hearts. He lives in our hearts and dwells in God. That is the only way God could share His presence with us. We are the church with many divisions, and Jesus Christ is within us. You decide whom you want to dominate your life, Jesus Christ or the seed of the serpent? It is all your choice! Making decisions is your choice. The church will come out of this and make the Son of God her own instead of the evil one.

The decisions of the church are up to the church, and the decisions of God are up to God and not man. We cannot change God in any way. He is Christ born to us as a Child and depending on your choice, He will be the Son given to us. The choice is in our nature, so is Jesus Christ. He had to choose between life and death, and He chose to die on the cross for life. It is our nature to think about things and assess them, whereby God make decisions and does not go back on His word; He accomplishes everything He sets out to do. He is in our nature as well—accomplishment.

We choose God not because of who He is but because He is in our nature (Genesis 2:7). We choose Him regardless, but making Jesus our choice becomes a problem because we do not know Him. But God says Jesus is in our nature. Jesus lives in our heart, and He is the Word of God in us. Jesus' nature is in us as a Child born to us, but to progress to a Son, a choice has to be made between you and God. You either choose God or yourself.

If you choose yourself, then you are with the evil one (the serpent) because he only comes in the form of man—flesh, the soil from the ground (Genesis 2:7). But the Spirit of God is in all of us, making us part of Him. If you choose Jesus Christ, you will be indebted to God, and He will honor all your needs according to His riches in Heaven, including righteousness. God will serve us as a kinsman. Eliminating God from the picture is like giving yourself up for the world (Luke 13: 28). Choose Jesus Christ for your peace!

How Did God Finish with the Church?

Jesus keeps on healing the church through His journey on earth. He is keeping the church healed and awake. God is going to birth the church from her roots and bring destruction to an end. The daughter of Jairus will awaken from her sleep and bring peace to the church on earth. Elevation will happen to the church on earth and will bring liberty to the people. Cleansing is needed in the church, and that will be done by Jesus as He did to the House of God in Jerusalem. All the animals will be driven out, and the tables of the moneychangers will be turned upside down. No more changing of people's mind in the church to suit mankind. All the principles will be based on the word of God in the church. The fight will still go on until all the principles are changed for good.

The crowd is almost caving in on Jesus, and crushing very fast and hard but the Lord is in control of the situation. He will not watch the crowd crush Him indefinitely. He is going to talk or act soon but time is a factor in all these. He will act at the right time and the right place which is the church; so, watch out preachers, teachers, leaders, pastors, prophets, etc.!

The Lord is coming, and soon, He will be with us. And as He did in the house of God in Jerusalem, He will do on earth in the churches. Sow the right seed! Time is not on our side regardless of when you read this. We do not have time on our side; we should cultivate the land that God has put us in charge of. Do not leave your talent hidden in the earth hoping for a miracle to happen; it will not happen. Sow your seed in good soil and cultivate your land for the harvest because the owner of the land is coming soon.

Do not leave your land uncultivated. Whatever talent God has given you, use it because the time is short. Clean the church of her mess and bring sanity to the church. Change the principles of the church to that of God. Wherever you find a principle changed, put it back where it is supposed to be. We are the laborers in the field working to bring this sanity to the church. Do not change your principles for that of the world. Live by God's principles and standards, and it shall be well with you. Without God's principles, we'll lack the faith in Christ, and without Christ, the church of God is lost. The church is in God's hand, and He directs her wherever He wants and restores her whenever He likes. This is a declaration that the Lord will come back again, but when? We do not know. What I know is, we should be in His field cultivating His land in peace and resurrecting the land that is dead in Jesus' name. Amen Church!

We are not going to get to the land of milk and honey until we unite and work together; so, no discrimination. Let's work together as a church to cleanse the land God has given to us. God will **restore** to the church everything lost and bring peace to her. He mentions that in Joel 2:25-32:

"I will give you back what you lost
in the years when swarms of locusts ate your crops.
It was I who sent this army against you.
Now you will have plenty to eat, and be satisfied.
You will praise the Lord your God,
who has done wonderful things for you.
My people will never be despised again.
Then, Israel, you will know that I am among you
and that I, the Lord, am your God
and there is no other.
My people will never be despised again.
"Afterward I will pour out my Spirit on everyone:
your sons and daughters will proclaim my message;
your old people will have dreams,
and your young people will see visions.
At that time I will pour out my Spirit
even on servants, both men and women.
"I will give warnings of that day
in the sky and on the earth;
there will be bloodshed, fire, and clouds of smoke.
The sun will be darkened,

and the moon will turn red as blood

before the great and terrible day of the Lord comes.

But all who ask the Lord for help will be saved.

As the Lord has said,

'Some in Jerusalem will escape;

those whom I choose will survive.'"

<u>My prayer</u>

I pray that we will acknowledge everyone and make our daily life a resolution to God's will. In Jesus' name, I pray. Amen.

What is the significance of the woman touching His servanthood garment?

- To obey all the commands of God.
- To preach the word of God to the world. In front of everyone who has denied not touching the garment of Jesus, she told the story of why she touched Jesus and how she was healed. She was a witness to the whole world of the goodness of God. She praised Jesus and worshipped Him in front of the entire crowd.

Psalm 12

Help us, Lord!
There is not a good person left;
honest people can no longer be found.
All of them lie to one another;
they deceive each other with flattery.
Silence those flattering tongues, O Lord!
Close those boastful mouths that say,
"With our words we get what we want.
We will say what we wish,
and no one can stop us."
"But now I will come," says the Lord,
"because the needy are oppressed
and the persecuted groan in pain.
I will give them the security they long for."
The promises of the Lord can be trusted;
they are as genuine as silver
refined seven times in the furnace.
The wicked are everywhere,
and everyone praises what is evil.
Keep us always safe, O Lord,
and preserve us from such people.

AUTHOR'S BIO

Eunice Forson is an ordained lay minister of the Gospel, author, and blogger with a calling to inspire others through the wisdom that was imparted upon her throughout her spiritual journey.

Over a decade ago, she welcomed Jesus into her life on her way to peace, purpose, and healing. Unable to find solace in the words of her fellow man, she turned to God who ultimately filled her soul with unconditional love and compassion.

Following Him and His ways from that point forward, she soon realized that she was placed on this earth to help others awaken to their God-given potential through the sacred power of words.

Eunice's forthcoming publication is a book series entitled *Discipline in the Church: The Plan of Perfect Intercession*. She also works as a pharmacist, earning her master's degree in pharmacy from the University of Portsmouth.